NEWPORT PUBLIC LIBRARY

P9-BZH-019

j920 Gra
Freedman, Russell
Martha Graham, a dancer's
NPT 31540002052403

DISCARD

Date Due

MAR 2 5 2002			
FEB 1 8 2003			
JUN 6 2003			

BRODART   Cat. No. 23 233   Printed in U.S.A.

NOV 1 6 2000

MARTHA GRAHAM

A DANCER'S LIFE

MARTHA GRAHAM

A DANCER'S LIFE

BY RUSSELL FREEDMAN

Newport Public Library

CLARION BOOKS
NEW YORK

j920 Gra
Freedman, Russell.
    Martha Graham, a dancer's
  NPT   31540002052403

CLARION

a Houghton Mifflin Company imprint
215 Park Avenue South, New York, NY 10003
Copyright © 1998 by Russell Freedman

Text is 12.5/17-point Garamond # 3.
Book design by Sylvia Frezzolini Severance.

All rights reserved.
For information about permission to reproduce selections from this book,
write to Permissions, Houghton Mifflin Company, 215 Park Avenue South,
New York, NY 10003.

Printed in the USA

LIBRARY OF CONGRESS CATALOGING-IN-PUBLICATION DATA

Freedman, Russell.
  Martha Graham: a dancer's life / by Russell Freedman.
     p.   cm.
Includes bibliographical references (p. 164) and index.
  Summary: a photobiography of the American dancer, teacher, and choreographer
who was born in Pittsburgh in 1895 and who became a leading figure in the
world of modern dance.
     ISBN 0-395-74655-8
1. Graham, Martha—Juvenile literature. 2. Women dancers—United States—
Biography—Juvenile literature. 3. Choreographers—United States—Biography—
Juvenile literature. 4. Modern dance—Juvenile literature. [1. Graham, Martha.
2. Dancers. 3. Choreographers. 4. Modern dance. 5. Women—Biography.]
  I. Title.
GV1785.G7F474   1998
792.8'028'092—dc21
   [B]   97-15832
                            CIP
                            AC

CRW   10 9 8 7 6 5 4 3 2

Frontis: Martha Graham in *Frontier*, 1935.
Photograph by Barbara Morgan.

3 1540 00205 2403

For Carolyn

Who understands a dancer's life

And for Maya and Deanna, who understand Carolyn

CONTENTS

That which cannot be spoken

can be sung,

That which cannot be sung

can be danced.

Old French saying

Martha Graham in *Serenata Morisca*, 1921.

CHAPTER ONE

ACROBATS OF GOD

AS AN AMBITIOUS YOUNG WOMAN who wanted to create a new kind of dance, Martha Graham spent many hours at New York City's Central Park Zoo. She would sit on a bench across from a lion in its cage and watch the animal pace back and forth, from one side of the cage to the other.

She was fascinated by the elemental power of the lion's great padding steps, by the purity of its movements. Again and again, it took four steps across the cage, turned in "a wonderful way," then took four steps back. "Finally, I learned how to walk that way," Graham recalled. "I learned from the lion the inevitability of return, the shifting of one's body."

Graham spent her very long life studying movement and challenging accepted ideas about what dance is and what a dancer can do. She looked upon dance as an exploration, a celebration of life, a religious calling that required absolute devotion. She called her dancers "acrobats of God" and told them, "Stand up! Keep your backs straight! Remember that this is where the wings grow."

One of the great American artists of the twentieth century, she was an electrifying performer and a deeply influential choreographer (the person who creates the steps, movements, and patterns of dances). "I don't call myself a choreographer, because that's a big, wonderful word that can cover up a lot of sins," she said. "I work. That's what I call what I do when I make dances."

Graham invented a revolutionary new language of dance, an original way of moving that she used to reveal the joys, passions, and sorrows common to all human experience. She had a genius for connecting movement with emotion. "Here was somebody who could manifest, make visible, all those feelings that you have inside you that you can't put words to," said Bertram Ross, one of her principal dancers.

For more than seventy years Graham danced, choreographed, and taught. She developed a distinctive system of training that could be taught to others, founded a school that has trained generations of dancers and choreographers, and changed the world of dance and dance theater for all time. The Martha Graham Dance Company is the world's oldest continuously performing modern dance troupe. And the Graham technique is used today by dance companies throughout the world.

Martha was a small, exotic-looking woman, almost tiny, but when she stepped behind the footlights, her magnetic stage presence made her seem larger than life. All she needed to do was to walk into a room, and all eyes were riveted upon her.

Bertram Ross never forgot his first visit to Graham's New York studio and the impression she made on him:

"At my very first class, she took a piece of chiffon and held it over her head and walked with it in this pattern she uses on the stage. She wanted to show us how dramatic just a plain walk could be.

"Now, I wasn't the first one who saw this. The girl I came to class with turned to me and whispered, 'Did you see that?' It was as if all the lights went out in the studio and a special spot came on. Her skin color changed, as though she were in a spotlight. All of a sudden, there was this energy, and she flushed. I've seen her do it many times since. She could control it, like blushing. It was spooky."

Graham triumphed as a dancer against the odds. While she had a comfortable childhood and a supportive family, she grew up in an environment that frowned on dancing as a career. When she began to study dance professionally at long last, she was considered too old, too short, too heavy, and too homely to be taken seriously. But she knew what she wanted to do, and

Martha Graham in *Letter to the World*, 1940. Photograph by Barbara Morgan.

she pursued her goal with the fierce intensity that marked her entire life.

Dance was her reason for living. Willing to risk everything, driven by a burning passion, she dedicated herself totally and absolutely to her art. "I did not choose to be a dancer," she often said. "I was chosen."

"When I first saw her company," dancer and choreographer Glen Tetley remembered, "I thought I was seeing a revelation. Time stopped for me. I could not believe what I was seeing. Those works are engraved on my brain, my mind, my heart. I've never forgotten, never, the atmosphere on stage, the lighting . . . the use of props, the use of costume . . . the strongest, simplest, most powerful theater I think I've ever seen."

Martha at age two.

CHAPTER TWO

BEWITCHED BY THE *G*ODDESS

SHE WAS A LITTLE GIRL. She stood looking up at her father, her hands clasped tightly before her, her cheeks burning with shame and humiliation.

"Martha," said her father, "you're not telling me the truth, are you?"

Martha's lips trembled. Tears welled in her eyes.

Kneeling down, her father put an arm around her. "Don't you know when you do something like this, I always know? There is always some movement that tells me you are deceiving me. You see, no matter what you say, you reveal yourself—you make fists you think I don't notice, your back gets very straight, maybe you shuffle your feet, your eyelids drop. Remember, Martha—movement never lies."

Long after she had forgotten what she lied about, Martha still remembered that awful moment and her father's words. Her movements had given her away—her hands, her feet, her eyes! It was as though her body had spoken. Looking back many years later, she said, "That was my very first lesson as a dancer."

Her father, George Greenfield Graham, was a family doctor with a keen interest in psychology. As a young medical-school graduate he had worked in a mental hospital, where he learned to analyze his patients as much by their actions as by their words. After marrying Jane Beers, he set up a private practice in Allegheny, Pennsylvania, a small town in the shadow of

Jennie Graham, Martha's mother, and George Greenfield Graham, Martha's father.

fast-growing Pittsburgh. The Grahams settled down in a spacious house. Dr. Graham's consulting rooms and dispensary were on the ground floor of his home, while the family's living quarters were upstairs.

Martha was born in this house on May 11, 1894, the eldest of three girls. Her sister Mary arrived in 1896, and the baby, Georgia, called Geordie, in 1900. A fourth child, a boy, died of scarlet fever before his second birthday.

George Graham was fifteen years older than his wife, a soft-spoken, doll-like woman known to everyone as Jennie. Martha would watch her father sweep her mother off the floor and carry her laughing up the stairs as Jennie's long black hair cascaded down about his strong arms.

Dr. Graham liked to gather his family around him while he played the piano and sang popular songs. A handsome man of great exuberance and charm, he was the grandson of an adventurous Irish immigrant who had arrived penniless in America, worked hard, and become president of Pittsburgh's first bank.

On her mother's side Martha traced her ancestry all the way back to Miles Standish and the Pilgrims who had arrived in America on the Mayflower. Her mother's people had been stern, God-fearing Puritan pioneers who had trekked west from the Atlantic seacoast to claim homesteads in what was then Indian territory—the rugged Allegheny Mountains.

The spirit of those Puritan ancestors was still very much alive in the Grahams' Allegheny household. Martha and her sisters were brought up strictly, with daily prayers, Sunday-school training, and regular attendance at their local Presbyterian church. The girls were expected to be polite, respectful, and obedient, to sit straight at the dinner table, to stand when spoken to by an adult, and to wear spotless white gloves when they went to church. As proper little ladies, they had to be ever mindful of their manners. In those straitlaced days called the Victorian age around the turn of the century, nothing, it seemed, was more important than good manners. Martha's maternal grandmother, who lived with the family, was fond of saying, "I would rather have a man with bad morals than with bad manners."

Martha had her mother's enormous deep-set eyes and glossy black hair. She had her father's independent spirit and, when she did not get her own way, his quick temper. "I was a very difficult child," she admitted. "I was quite stubborn and willful even then."

As the eldest sister, the bossiest, and the most adventuresome, Martha ruled the girls' upstairs playroom. She was the ringleader, the one who told Mary and Geordie what to do and when to do it.

Joining the girls in their games, sharing their secrets, and keeping them strictly in line was Elizabeth Prendergast, an Irish immigrant girl who had come into the household as a nurse, nanny, cook, and maid shortly after Martha was born. Martha adored Lizzie. While Lizzie had never gone to school, she told wonderful stories right out of her head, spinning fantasies and folktales in her lilting Irish brogue. Lizzie loved the theater and went to plays and musicals on her days off. She liked to sit on the floor with the

Martha and her younger sister, Mary, with their nanny Lizzie Prendergast.

three girls and in her sweet, lovely voice sing songs from the popular shows of the day.

Martha and her sisters had never been inside a real theater, but with Lizzie's help they made up plays and entertainments of their own. Wearing scarves, veils, and costumes that their mother had sewn for them, and festooned with junk jewelry, the girls turned their playroom into a make-believe theater.

Once, Martha surprised everyone in the family by inviting them into

Martha with
her youngest
sister, Geordie.

her room at a certain hour to attend a show she had made up by herself. She had rigged a bedsheet from one end of the room to the other as a curtain. When the curtain was drawn, she stood there alone and sang her big number, a tricky rhyming tune that Lizzie had taught her. "I always wanted to go on the stage," she said many years later. "I knew there was a magic someplace in the world that had to do with the stage."

Lizzie was a devout Roman Catholic, and she would sometimes take the Graham sisters to church with her. Martha was entranced by the music and rituals of that church, "a place of ceremony, mystery, and blessing," she wrote. She loved the chanting and processionals, the lighted candles at the altars, the tall statues of kindly saints. In years to come the colorful pageantry of the holy rites she had witnessed as a child and kept in her memory would influence the dances she created as an adult.

Allegheny was in the heart of the Pennsylvania coal country, a stone's throw from the fiery, smoke-spewing factories and steel mills of industrial

Pittsburgh, which would soon swallow up the smaller town. Martha would remember her hometown as a bleak, gray place, "spun entirely out of evening and dark thread," where everything seemed to be covered in coal dust and soot.

Her sister Mary suffered from chronic asthma. As Mary's attacks grew worse, the Grahams decided that she needed a change of climate. In 1908, when Martha was fourteen, Dr. Graham moved his family to California, a six-day journey by train. They settled in Santa Barbara, a sunny seacoast town north of Los Angeles known for its flower gardens, blue skies, and fresh ocean breezes.

Martha and her sisters reveled in the sunlight and open spaces of Santa Barbara. Not far from their house was a broad, flat-topped cliff overlooking the Pacific Ocean. The girls would stand at the edge of the cliff, watching the crashing waves down below and breathing in the sea air. Then, with arms spread wide, they would start to run wildly, racing across the high plateau, leaping and bounding, their loose hair flying in the breeze. "Freedom! I ran. I fell down. I got up. I ran again," Martha remembered.

She quickly made a place for herself at Santa Barbara High, which at the time was small by today's standards. Martha's class of forty was one of the largest the school had ever had. A fast learner and an avid reader, Martha became an editor of *Olive and Gold*, the school's literary magazine. Encouraged by her teachers, who felt that she had a special gift for words and language, she wrote short stories and a two-scene play, a comedy set in the girls' locker room. Strongly athletic, she joined the girls' basketball team, wearing her hair in a single braid that swung back and forth as she dribbled across the gymnasium floor in bloomers and middy blouse. And she enrolled in a sewing class, surprising her mother and herself by becoming an accomplished seamstress. Soon she was able to cut and sew her own dresses.

By the time she was sixteen, Martha, at five foot two, had reached almost her full height. She had a strong, straight body, a slender neck, and black hair as shiny as a cat's fur. And while she moved with self-assurance, took pride in her skills, and enjoyed parties and school dances, she was known more for her quiet determination than for good looks. She considered her sisters beautiful and thought of herself as plain-looking and shy. "I was not the pretty one," she recalled.

One day she was walking with her parents down a Santa Barbara street when a poster in a shop window caught her eye. She turned back for a second look. Pictured on the poster was a beautiful, richly bejeweled woman sitting cross-legged on a small thronelike platform. Her eyes were half lowered. On her lips was the mysterious hint of a smile. She was a famous dancer named Ruth St. Denis, dressed for her role as the Hindu goddess Radha. The poster announced that she would be performing at the Mason Opera House in Los Angeles from April 24 to 29, 1911.

Martha stared at the poster transfixed, studying every detail of Ruth St. Denis's costume and appearance. Then she ran ahead to catch up with her parents. She pleaded with them to let her attend one of the dancer's performances. Dr. Graham traveled to Los Angeles often, and he agreed to take Martha with him. He made a special occasion of the event, buying her a new dress and hat and giving her a corsage of violets, which she saved and treasured for many years.

Ruth St. Denis was one of the great dancers of the time. Before seeing the poster, however, Martha had never heard of her. In fact, she had never attended a dance concert of any kind until that warm spring evening when the curtain rose in the Mason Opera House.

Miss St. Denis appeared onstage barefoot. Wearing colorful storybook costumes, she presented a program of exotic dances that hinted of the mysterious East. In her celebrated solo *The Incense* her rippling body seemed to become one with the smoke of burning incense wafting upward toward the heavens. In *The Cobra* her long sinuous arms became two coiling, writhing snakes winding around her body and neck, while the rings on her fingers shone like the serpents' glowing eyes. In *Radha*, named for the Hindu goddess pictured on the poster, St. Denis evoked the five human senses, speaking not in words but through expressive movements and alluring gestures about the earthly delights of sight, smell, sound, taste, and touch.

Martha sat spellbound through the performance, bewitched by the

Ruth St. Denis, dressed for her role as the goddess Radha.
Photograph by Otto Sarony.

magical theater of Ruth St. Denis. "From that moment on," she recalled, "my fate was sealed. I couldn't wait to learn to dance as the goddess did."

Up to then she had had no dance training at all, but she had found an idol, an ideal to strive toward. She was going to be a dancer like Ruth St. Denis. As far as her parents were concerned, this sudden new interest was nothing more than a whim, a passing fancy. To the respectable Grahams, dancing professionally on the stage was not an acceptable career for a proper young lady. Dr. Graham expected Martha to go to college, preferably to Vassar, where his own mother had studied. After college, he expected, his daughter would marry and raise a family.

Ruth St. Denis as she appeared on souvenir postcards around 1908. Since there were no instantaneous photographs at the time, she had to hold her pose for several seconds. The points of her skirt are pulled back by wires, but it is her artistry that creates a sense of motion.

Martha still had two years of high school left. She dropped basketball, because she did not want to injure the legs that were now dedicated to dancing. In place of sports she took up dramatics, winning leading roles in both her junior and senior class plays. As a senior she was appointed editor-in-chief of the graduation issue of *Olive and Gold*. She joined the debating society and the drama club and took part in other school activities. As vice-president of the student council, she was photographed looking very serious and purposeful, her hair parted severely in the middle.

The excitement of her class plays had only strengthened her resolve to go on the stage. When she graduated from Santa Barbara High in June 1913, she told her parents that she did not want to attend Vassar or any other academic college, as her father had in mind. She had heard about a

Martha at the time of her high school graduation.

place in Los Angeles called the Cumnock School of Expression, an experimental junior college where young people with theatrical ambitions could study both academic subjects and practical theater arts. George and Jennie Graham knew by now that their headstrong eldest daughter had a mind of her own. Martha persuaded them to let her go down to Los Angeles with her friend Marguerite Andrus, another girl from Santa Barbara, and enroll in Cumnock.

Martha was nineteen. With her usual seriousness she took courses in art and literature, along with acting, playwriting, stage lighting, and for the first time dancing. Three times a week she joined a class in "dance expression," a kind of rhythmic, fluid movement also called "interpretive" or "esthetic" dancing. She and Marguerite lived in the school's dormitory under the supervision of a housemother. On weekends and holidays they rode the train home to Santa Barbara.

A year after she entered Cumnock, Martha's father died unexpectedly of a heart attack. "Suddenly our whole world shifted," she recalled. "We were left a house of women—mother, Lizzie, Geordie, Mary, and myself." While Dr. Graham did not leave a great deal of money, Martha's mother was determined to budget carefully and see to it that her daughters completed their educations.

Martha spent three years at Cumnock, graduating just after her twenty-second birthday in 1916. She had already decided on her next move. Her idol, Ruth St. Denis, had opened a dance school in Los Angeles with her young dancer-husband, Ted Shawn. Five years after first seeing the "goddess" dance, Martha mustered her courage and applied for admission to the Ruth St. Denis School of Dancing and Related Arts, better known as Denishawn.

With her father gone, Martha felt free to chart her own future course. She felt that her mother was intrigued by the idea. "She became very excited about my wanting to be a dancer," Martha wrote.

Charles Weidman and Martha Graham in *Danse Arabe*, 1921.

CHAPTER THREE

GOING TO THE *Top*

MARTHA HAD MADE UP her mind to become a dancer, but she seemed a very unlikely prospect. Many future dance performers start serious study by the time they are nine or ten. Martha was twenty-two. Short and intense, she looked as serious as an owl. She had put on weight since her high school days, perhaps more than her slight frame could bear, and she still thought of herself as plain.

Every aspiring student had to appear for an audition with "Miss Ruth," as the students called Ruth St. Denis. Martha was ushered into a studio where a large man in shirt sleeves sat at a piano, smoking a cigar and reading a detective novel. He nodded at her. Martha waited. Finally Miss Ruth appeared, a tall, elegant woman wearing a long, flowing dress that billowed around her as she glided into the room. Her face was framed by a halo of prematurely white hair. She sat on a small bench, arranged her skirt around her ankles, and smiled. "Now, dance for me," she said.

At the piano Louis Horst put down his novel and began to play a waltz. Martha was terrified. Relying on her lessons in "dance expression" at the Cumnock School, she raised her arms, lifted her feet, and began to move about the room.

Miss Ruth was not impressed. When the music stopped, she thanked Martha, but she had already decided to turn this unpromising new student over to her husband, Ted Shawn. "You take her in your classes, Teddy dear," she told him. "I don't know what to do with her."

"She was quite a few years above the average age of all the other girls in the school," Shawn recalled. "Let's admit that she was homely, and Martha was overweight. I won't say exactly fat, but she was dumpy, unprepossessing."

Nevertheless, Martha was allowed to enroll at Denishawn. For the moment she was happy to study, practice, and be near her idol, Miss Ruth.

Ruth St. Denis had been acclaimed in both Europe and America as one of the great dancers of the age. Along with Isadora Duncan, another famous American, she was changing the way people thought about dancers and the dance. These two charismatic women were creating a new kind of dance, totally different from classical ballet and having little in common with ballroom dancing or with the popular tap, soft shoe, or clog dancing of vaudeville acts and variety shows. They were among the first to lead dance into the modern era, and the first nonclassical dancers to be recognized as serious artists.

St. Denis had grown up on a New Jersey farm and started her career as a high-kicking vaudeville dancer. Wanting to do more artistic work, she turned for inspiration to the dance practices and mysticism of Egypt, India, and the Far East. Like Isadora Duncan, St. Denis rejected the prescribed steps and geometrical arrangements of ballet in favor of a lush, expressive barefoot style. She sought to capture the world of pure spirit when she performed, and she regarded her dancing body as an "instrument of spiritual revelation."

Miss Ruth was thirteen years older than her husband, Ted, a former divinity student who had vowed to become a dancer himself after seeing St. Denis perform. The school they founded together was unique, one of the first professional schools of dance in America. While students learned basic ballet techniques, they also took classes in Oriental dance, Spanish dance, American Indian dance, and just about any other form of rhythmic movement that caught the fancy of Miss Ruth and Ted Shawn.

The school occupied a big Spanish-style mansion surrounded by euca-

Ruth St. Denis lectures to a class of Denishawn dancers. Martha is seated in the front row, second from the right.

lyptus trees atop a hill in the heart of Los Angeles. Pet peacocks roamed the grounds. Tennis courts had been converted into a big outdoor studio, shaded from the sun and shielded from rain by billowing white canopies.

Students came to Denishawn from all over the country. Along with classes in ballet and ethnic dance, they took courses in music, dramatic gesture, lighting, makeup, and costume design. They attended lectures on the history and philosophy of dance, joined discussions on Oriental art and Greek philosophy, and had sessions in yoga and meditation conducted by Miss Ruth wearing one of her many saris as the students sat at her feet. There was even a class in the art of posing for photographs, a critical skill for any would-be performer.

Denishawn was not only a residential school but a highly successful performing dance company as well. Professional dancers trained by the school toured the country, appearing in dance concerts, on vaudeville stages, in silent movies, and in elaborate spectacles such as *A Dance Pageant of Egypt,*

Greece, and India. Soon after entering Denishawn, Martha Graham made her professional debut as a minor member of the chorus when that vast pageant was presented at the Greek Theater in Berkeley, California, with a huge cast and a forty-piece orchestra.

Despite her unpromising audition, Martha surprised both Miss Ruth and Ted Shawn with her determination to learn and her quick mastery of difficult exercises, gestures, and steps. "She was exceedingly quiet and shy," St. Denis recalled. "Most of the time in my class she sat very still and listened."

Martha makes her Denishawn debut as Priestess of Isis in *A Dance Pageant of Egypt, Greece, and India,* 1916.

Martha would go to the studio alone in the evening and practice by herself, dancing far into the night, "trying to find strange, beautiful movements of my own." She enjoyed the discipline, the regimen of training, and the growing satisfaction of seeing her body become trim and strong, a supple instrument that could respond instantly to her commands.

At the end of her first year at Denishawn, she was recruited to demonstrate basic movements in Miss Ruth's classes. Then she was entrusted with teaching duties in dance classes for children, some of them only three or four years old. She continued to appear as a member of the Denishawn Company chorus, but she wasn't considered ready to perform the company's repertory. "They thought I was good enough to be a teacher, but not a dancer," she recalled.

She would sit quietly in a corner and watch advanced students practice. One day Shawn and some students were rehearsing a Moorish gypsy dance called *Serenata Morisca*. He was trying to decide which dancer would perform the solo on the road. They went over it again and again, but Shawn wasn't satisfied. He glanced over at Martha, with her straight black hair and high cheekbones, and said, "It's too bad Martha doesn't know this dance. She would look just right in it."

"But I do know it," Martha protested.

"That's impossible," said Shawn. "You've never danced it!"

Martha rose to her feet, stepped out to the middle of the studio, and as Shawn watched in amazement, proved that she had mastered the difficult dance simply by watching others perform it.

Her performance was so convincing, Shawn immediately made her one of his leading dancers. From then on she performed *Serenata Morisca* regularly onstage.

Impressed with Martha's talent, Shawn created a dramatic new dance-drama as a starring vehicle for her. *Xochitl* told the story of a beautiful Toltec Indian maiden who dances ferociously to protect her virtue against the drunken advances of the Toltec emperor. Martha certainly looked the part, and as she fought off the emperor, she danced with a fiery conviction that brought audiences to their feet.

(right) *Xochitl* poster for the Pantages Circuit season, 1920–21. (below) Martha Graham as the Toltec maiden Xochitl: "a wild, beautiful creature."

Xochitl was a huge success. Martha performed the dance in Denishawn Company productions across America and eventually in London. Shawn himself frequently danced the role of the emperor. He never forgot Martha's wild fury as she portrayed the Toltec maiden. "Sometimes my face would be bleeding when I came offstage," he said. "Once she punched me so hard that there was a hole under my lip right through to my teeth."

"I was like an animal in my movements," Martha recalled. "I wanted to be a wild, beautiful creature, maybe of another world—but very, very wild."

By 1921 Martha was touring the country regularly as a featured soloist with America's leading dance company. Traveling by train, the dancers performed in big cities and small towns from coast to coast. They gave three performances a day on weekdays, and four on Saturdays and Sundays. A typical program consisted of twenty-one numbers, including several solos for Martha. Backstage, the dancers were constantly diving in and out of their elaborate costumes.

These tours gave Martha the stage experience she craved and her first taste of fame. In the state of Washington the *Tacoma New Tribune* called her "a brilliant young dancer." And when a Denishawn touring troupe arrived in Santa Barbara, she was interviewed by a reporter from the *Santa Barbara News.* "I could not do anything that I could not feel," Martha said. "A dance must dominate me completely, until I lose sense of anything else."

Before long Martha was made manager of one of Denishawn's touring companies. When the troupe went on the road without Ted or Miss Ruth, Martha was in charge. In addition to being star soloist, she was now responsible for the group's railroad tickets, hotel reservations, paychecks, and costumes. She proved to be a demanding taskmistress. She was determined not to let repetition lower the dancers' standards as they performed the same numbers again and again during one-night stands. "She would take out easy steps and put in more interesting ones every so often," dancer Anne Douglas remembered. "With several shows a day, it kept us from getting stale."

Martha was a perfectionist. And she was temperamental. When things did not go exactly as she wished, she sometimes exploded. Once during a tour she put in a long-distance call to Shawn in Los Angeles and told him

Denishawn dancers on tour in Charleston, South Carolina, 1922. Ruth St. Denis and Ted Shawn stand at the top of the stairs. Martha is directly to St. Denis's right.

that she wanted to add a new dance to the program. He replied that it couldn't be done. Absolutely not! Martha insisted. Shawn refused. In a rage, Martha ripped the backstage telephone off the wall and threw it on the floor. "I had a very bad temper, very bad," she admitted years later. "I still have it, though I do not use it often. But I can use it, if need be, on occasion."

Shawn had a temper equal to Martha's. At lunch one day in a New York restaurant, they argued over Martha's teaching duties. She felt that Ted was being unreasonable. Suddenly she stood up, grabbed the tablecloth, and pulled it—along with all the dishes, silver, and food—off the table and onto the floor. Then she stormed out of the restaurant and hailed a taxi. As she was getting in, Shawn caught up with her. "I don't ever want to see you

Dancing a tango with Ted Shawn.

again in my life," he screamed. "And I mean it!" Then he slammed the taxi door so hard, the window fell out and shattered on the street.

The next day they made up.

During Denishawn's cross-country tours, Martha spent a great deal of time with Louis Horst, the company's music director, "this huge, great-spirited musician and composer," as she called him. A broad-shouldered bear of a man who like Miss Ruth had prematurely white hair, Louis was ten years older than Martha. He was separated from his wife, Betty, a former Denishawn dancer who had moved to San Francisco. He had a dry wit, a wide knowledge of literature and philosophy, and a warm appreciation of dancers, whom he considered the most beautiful people on earth. He said that he could never think of loving a woman who wasn't a dancer, and who couldn't dance well. He had watched Martha grow from a shy, awkward student into a striking young woman and self-confident performer, and he was captivated by her blazing intensity.

Martha admired Louis's fine musicianship and his brilliant mind. "He

With Louis Horst in the Denishawn studio, around 1923.

encouraged all the different dancers to be their best," she wrote. "He would not tolerate mediocrity." During long train trips they spent hours talking about books, music, and ideas, and confiding in each other. Martha looked to Louis for guidance and advice, for strength. They became devoted friends. She listened to Louis with her heart, and in time she fell in love with him.

"Louis brought me out," she recalled. "He saw me as something strange and different. He schooled me in certain behavior, discipline and a deep respect for music. . . . He had the most to do with shaping my early life."

Denishawn gave Martha plenty of opportunities to teach, learn, travel, and perform, but she was growing restless. Miss Ruth and Ted were having marital problems, and Martha was often summoned to help make peace between them. Miss Ruth, meanwhile, had insisted on taking over some of Martha's roles. Martha was tired of the company's rivalries and intrigues. Beyond that, she was weary of performing the same exotic dances over and over again—dances inspired by foreign cultures and staged by Ted Shawn. She felt that Shawn had nothing else to teach her. And while she would always admire Miss Ruth and her spiritual approach to dance, she wanted to find her own way. She was ready for a change.

Her chance came in 1923, when she was offered a job as a featured soloist in the *Greenwich Village Follies*, a popular Broadway musical and comedy revue. John Murray Anderson, the show's producer, had seen Martha dance and wanted to hire her. Louis was thinking of leaving Denishawn also. He wanted to travel to Europe and study the latest trends in contemporary music. He urged Martha to take the new job. After seven years with Denishawn, she broke away and moved to New York.

Because the *Follies* ran on Broadway year after year, performers were constantly changing their acts, adding new material for each new edition of the revue. Martha now had a chance to create dances of her own, but Anderson, the producer, insisted that she stick closely to the tried-and-true Denishawn formula. He wanted her to wear fanciful ethnic costumes and perform dances like *Serenata Morisca* that suggested the mystery and romance of distant lands. Even so, he regarded Martha as a "class act." He felt that she was

Star of the
*Greenwich
Village
Follies*.
Photograph by
Nikolas Muray.

an artist, while his other female dancers, who paraded about in sexy costumes and towering feathered headdresses, were simply showgirls.

As a featured *Follies* soloist, Martha became a Broadway star overnight, dancing four solos at every show and bringing down the house. She toured the country with the *Follies*, performed in London, had many admirers, and earned $350 a week, a fortune in those days.

She seemed to be leading a glamorous life, but she wasn't happy. Except for the money, dancing in the *Follies* wasn't so different from dancing for Denishawn, and that was not what she wanted for herself. She sent most of her salary home to her mother in Santa Barbara, lived simply in a small Greenwich Village apartment, went to plays and concerts whenever she could, saw a few friends, and wrote long letters to Louis in Europe. "The *Follies* served a purpose," she wrote, "but I knew that there was something else for me to do."

After two seasons with the *Follies* Martha left to discover her own kind of dance. She was thirty years old. Time was rushing past. "I'm going to the top," she told a friend. "Nothing is going to stop me. And I shall do it alone."

Martha Graham (center) with two members of her first dance group,
Evelyn Sabin (left) and Betty MacDonald (right).

CHAPTER FOUR

#

TO SUPPORT HERSELF, MARTHA turned to teaching. She became codirector of a new dance department at the Eastman School of Music in Rochester, New York. She would have a studio to work in, students to train, and opportunities to choreograph—"a word I never heard of until I reached New York. At Denishawn, we just made up dances."

Every week she commuted by overnight train from New York City to Rochester, more than 350 miles away. She spent three days teaching at Eastman, then took the train back to New York for a second teaching job at the John Murray Anderson–Robert Milton School of Theater Arts, where she trained performers for Anderson's musical revues. Meanwhile, she opened her own New York City dance studio, renting a long, narrow room at Carnegie Hall where she taught a small group of private students.

Free at last from the demands of show business, Martha wanted to develop her own personal dance style. She wasn't sure what form that style would take, but she knew it would be something new, something startling, perhaps, a dance style in tune with the times.

During one of her cross-country tours she had visited the Art Institute of Chicago and seen an abstract painting by the Russian artist Wassily Kandinsky: a bold slash of red running across a field of blue. It was one of the first modern paintings she had ever seen, and she was struck by its vibrant beauty and dynamic sense of movement. "I nearly fainted because at that moment I knew I was not mad, that others saw the world, saw art, the way I did. . . . I said, 'I will do that someday. I will make a dance like that.'"

Soon after she started teaching, Louis returned from Europe, bringing word of exciting new developments in the worlds of music and dance. "I began talking to Martha," he recalled, "I said, 'There are new things happening, and you've got to start now. You've got to start breaking away from Denishawn.'

"'Well, I'm trying to,' she said. And she began working out new exercises, new dances. She would come down from Rochester every week and we'd talk and rehearse."

From among her students at Eastman Martha selected three talented young women to become her first dance group. After six months of training and drilling, they were ready to go on the stage.

"We had something like nineteen dollars between us," Louis remembered. Borrowing a thousand dollars from a friend, they rented a Broadway theater for one evening. On April 18, 1926, Martha's little company, billed as "Martha Graham and Dance Group," made its debut. "I wanted to gamble on being judged on Broadway, and not perform in my studio just for friends," she said.

She had choreographed an evening-long program of eighteen short dances. Martha had designed and sewn the costumes with the help of her three dancers, and she had created the lighting effects. Louis accompanied the dancers on the piano. Although it snowed that night, Martha attracted a big-enough audience to pay both the theater rental and her debt. "They came because I was such a curiosity—a woman who could do her own work," she said.

Most of the dances, with titles like *The Three Gopi Maidens, Maid with the Flaxen Hair*, and *Clair de Lune*, were reminiscent of her Denishawn days, though there were sparks of freshness and originality. Newspaper critics found Martha and her trio of dancers "decorative, pretty and undisturbing," and "exotically graceful." Graham herself would later describe those early dances as "childish things, dreadful."

Martha in *Desir* . . .

. . . and *Tanagra*,
two dances from her
first independent
concert in 1926.
Photographs by
Soichi Sunami.

She was already planning for her second dance concert. In the next few years her dances would prove as daring and innovative as the Kandinsky painting she so admired. From 1926 through 1930 she created seventy-nine new dances for herself and her Dance Group. Many of those dances broke new ground.

In 1927 she stunned her audience with a short solo called *Revolt*, a dance that was anything but "decorative, pretty and undisturbing." *Revolt* was Martha's first dance of social protest, a stark, forceful comment on injustice and the outraged human spirit. Those who saw the dance described it as a powerful manifesto, a call to arms, in which the dancer, body braced, elbows jutting, seemed to be fighting some sinister but invisible force.

In 1928 Martha expressed her social conscience again in the moving solo *Immigrant* and in the antiwar *Poems of 1917*. In 1929 *Adolescence* explored the fears and desires of a young girl. *Dance,* the same year, emphasized pure movement, what Martha called "strong, free, joyous action." Wearing a red dress, she kept her feet planted on a small platform and moved mainly between her shoulders and her knees. She seemed to be dancing from deep inside her gut, as though she were detonating depth charges that pulsated and sent vibrations through her body and out into the surrounding air.

"With these dances, she really began to break out," Horst recalled. Martha was learning to express deep-seated feelings and strong convictions through the dynamic language of dance. Her classes became experimental laboratories where she began to develop a radically new way of dancing. "I can't explain how she developed it," Horst said in an interview in 1960. "She just worked on technique. She discovered a lot of new movements. And she just kept working and finding. She does it still, you know, she changes her technique every few years. There's always something new that she brings in."

Martha left her job with Eastman in 1927 and began a long association with New York City's Neighborhood Playhouse, where she taught aspiring actors how to move onstage. Meanwhile, she opened a new dance studio in Greenwich Village, the vibrant Manhattan neighborhood that was in its

With works
like *Revolt*
in 1927 . . .

. . . and *Adolescence*
in 1929, Graham was
creating a new language
of dance.

Photographs by
Soichi Sunami.

heyday as a haven for writers, artists, intellectuals, and bohemians. The new studio served as Martha's classroom, workshop, and home. A tiny bedroom and kitchenette were tucked away in the rear. The one large room, used for classes and rehearsals, was bare except for Louis's piano in one corner, and a drum with a mallet nearby.

Louis was the accompanist for Martha's classes and taught with her at the Neighborhood Playhouse. "What a disciplinarian he was!" dancer Marie Marchowsky remembered. "He'd sit at the piano smoking his cigar, and, although his hooded eyes appeared to be closed, he didn't miss a thing. We called him 'Eagle Eye.'" At times Louis would get up from the piano to help Martha demonstrate, his little feet and great bulk skipping across the studio floor.

He had his own small apartment a couple of blocks away, but he and Martha saw each other every day. "We were always together," he recalled. "We ate our meals together, and we always rehearsed every night at the studio. We didn't have money to go to the theater or concerts very often."

Teaching part-time at the Neighborhood Playhouse, and with just a few private students of her own, Martha had a hard time making ends meet. Often she had to borrow twenty-five or fifty cents from Louis to get through the day, at a time when the subway cost five cents and a cup of coffee ten. Louis was in demand as a pianist and music director for other dancers and dance companies, and he took all the work he could get to spare Martha the need for a full-time job. He kept track of his loans to Martha in a notebook, and when she gave a concert, she paid up and they started anew. She did her own laundry, made her own clothes, and became a vegetarian to save money on meals. She was poor, but she didn't mind. She was doing exactly what she wanted to do.

Along with Graham, other gifted young dancers and choreographers were also rebelling against the conventions of the past and forging unique styles of their own. Those working in New York included Doris Humphrey and her partner, Charles Weidman, former dancers with Martha at Denishawn; Helen Tamiris, who had a special interest in jazz and spirituals; Agnes de Mille, a niece of the famous movie director Cecil B. De Mille; and a number of others. They were all creating new dances and attending one another's dance recitals.

"This was a stirring period in American dance history—a period of revolution and adventure," wrote de Mille. "We all turned out en bloc for every occasion, wrangling and fighting in the lobbies, as though at a political meeting. . . . We risked everything; every one of us had thrown overboard all of our tradition."

The 1920s were a decade of experimentation in all the arts—in painting, music, literature, and the theater—and this new breed of young dancers wanted to speak for the changing times in which they lived. They weren't content to imitate the exotic dances of Ruth St. Denis or the Greek interpretations of Isadora Duncan. And while they respected classical ballet as an art, they felt that it could never say enough about the pressing concerns of contemporary life.

Classical ballet dated back more than three hundred years to its origins as an elegant spectacle in the royal courts of Europe. With its five basic positions of the feet, prescribed positions of the body, and geometric relationships among the dancers, ballet was a highly controlled dance form, characterized by grace and precision of movement. While there were no major American ballet companies during the 1920s, polished troupes from Europe toured the country from time to time, featuring lavish productions and famous stars such as Anna Pavlova. To the rebellious young American dancers of the time, traditional European ballet seemed decadent and undemocratic. They regarded its dashing princes and dying swans as escapist and antiquated, and its elaborate formal technique as artificial and restricting.

Martha Graham and her fellow dance pioneers were ready to discard all the old rules. They wanted to create a new kind of dance, a uniquely American dance that would capture the spirit and energy of their country and their times.

In place of ballet's fanciful stories they explored serious themes dealing with ordinary people and modern life. They did away with glamorous costumes and scenery and danced in simple outfits on bare stages. Instead of soaring gracefully through space, they introduced spare, stark, angular

Anna Pavlova, the most famous ballerina of the early twentieth century.

Martha Graham in *Immigrant: Steerage, Strike*, 1928. Photograph by Soichi Sunami.

movements, blunt gestures, and stern facial expressions as they sought to lay bare fundamental human moods and feelings. Their dances were meant to be challenging and disturbing.

Because this new kind of dance dealt with modern concerns, it came to be called "modern dance," a term the dancers themselves never liked. Graham detested labels of any kind, but when pressed, she called her work "contemporary dance" and her individual dances "ballets."

All these dance pioneers were working independently as they developed their distinctive personal styles. Like Martha, they had their own students and their own studios. They sat hawk-eyed through the dance concerts of their rivals, but for the most part they did not mingle. "They were experimenting in different ways," said Horst, "but they were all doing modern dance."

At her Greenwich Village studio Martha held daytime classes for paying students and evening-long rehearsals for her chosen company of performing dancers called the Group, which now numbered twelve women. They were all devoted Graham disciples who had seen Martha perform and had fallen under her spell. Gertrude Shurr had attended Martha's early dance concerts in 1926 and 1927. "All I can remember is how beautiful the concerts were," she recalled. "I cried. I wanted to dance like Martha. . . . All I knew was that I wanted to study with her and dance in her company."

Many members of the Group would make dance their lifelong profession. During the day they worked as secretaries, salesclerks, waitresses, and artists' models, but no job was allowed to interfere with Martha's evening rehearsals, which sometimes lasted until one or two in the morning. They were paid ten dollars for a performance and nothing at all for the months of rehearsals that often preceded a performance. "We didn't expect to be paid," Nelle Fisher recalled. "We almost didn't want to be, because, you know, it was complete dedication, like a sisterhood."

Louis served as Martha's accompanist, musical director, collaborator, and trusted adviser. He took Martha to baseball games and prizefights, introduced her to the newest ideas in philosophy and psychology and the latest trends in European and American music, and composed music for her dances. With Louis she could share her dreams, confide her doubts, and test her wildest ideas. He was her sounding board.

Louis had been the first to recognize genius in Martha, and he was the one person who could deal with her dark moods and temperamental outbursts when the work at hand did not measure up to her expectations. "When she's down she gets what the Irish call 'the glooms,'" he once said. "Yes, the real glooms. Then she'd get over them and say 'I'm sorry, Louis. I don't know how you put up with me. Do forgive me.'"

Back in their Denishawn days Louis had nicknamed her "Mirthless Martha." He would cheer her up when she was depressed by playing Scott Joplin's lilting ragtime tunes on his piano. "Oh, Louis," Martha would plead, "play me the 'Maple Leaf Rag.'" And as he did, her gloomy face would break into a smile.

In 1929 Martha Graham and Dance Group gave the first performance of *Heretic,* regarded today as her earliest major work. Dressed in white, and with loose, flowing hair, Martha danced in opposition to a double row of women clad in black Puritan garb, their hair drawn straight back and knotted, their stern faces set like white masks. Again and again the solitary heretic in white struggles to advance, trying to break through a barrier formed by the women in black. But each time they move rigidly in unison, blocking her way like automatons, as their bare feet slam down onto the floor. Some of the dancers lunge at the heretic, some seem to be spitting at her, while others turn their backs. At the end, her spirit broken, the outcast sinks to the floor, defeated by her oppressors.

Heretic was meant to be provocative. John Martin, then the dance critic of *The New York Times*, called the work "strikingly original and glowing with vitality." Made up of blunt, forceful movements and stark gestures, with an old Breton folk tune repeated again and again as its musical background, the dance can be seen as a powerful condemnation of intolerance, especially toward people who are different in some way—a theme that Graham would return to again. "To many people, I was a heretic," she wrote. "I did not dance the way that other people danced. . . . In many ways, I showed onstage what most people came to the theater to avoid."

Martha Graham and Dance Group in *Heretic*, 1929. Photograph by Soichi Sunami.

"Audiences who come to be amused and entertained will go away disappointed, for Miss Graham's programs are alive with passion and protest," wrote John Martin. "She does the unforgivable thing for a dancer to do—she makes you think."

This new kind of dance wasn't to everyone's liking. It was neither beautiful nor romantic. Some critics complained that Graham's spare, stark, unsmiling dance style seemed tortured and distorted. One critic, Stark Young, wrote: "She looks as though she were about to give birth to a cube."

Martha and her fellow "modern" dancers were often the butt of ridicule and hostile jokes. Women in America had won the right to vote only a few years earlier, in 1920, and many people were still uncomfortable with the image of the "new woman" who sought a career, spoke out on social issues, and went knowledgeably to the polls. It was all right to be a high-kicking, scantily clad chorus girl, but a woman who ran a dance company and created works that commented on war, poverty, and intolerance seemed unnatural and suspicious.

Martha's work was so startlingly different, people did not always know how to react. After one of her early recitals, an actress friend from her Denishawn days went backstage and said, "Martha, dear, how long do you expect to keep up this dreadful dancing?"

"As long as I have an audience," Martha replied.

"I wanted people to like me," she said later, "but I had to dance what I was compelled to do and if the public hated me, well . . . I'd rather have them hate me than be indifferent to me."

Graham
exercises
demonstrated
by Nina
Caiserman,
1942.
Photographs by
Barbara Morgan.

CHAPTER FIVE

CREATING A NEW LANGUAGE OF *D*ANCE

MARTHA GRAHAM'S CLASSES ALWAYS began down on the floor. Sitting, kneeling, or lying on the studio's bare wood floor, her students—all women in the early days—performed a series of warming-up exercises designed to stretch their spines and strengthen their back and leg muscles.

Wearing tank suits, the women worked in silence, stretching and bending, breathing in and breathing out, concentrating on each movement with great intensity. Martha walked among them, coaxing, correcting, encouraging. "Don't just lean on the floor," she would say, "push *down* against it to give it more strength to your movements." Her husky voice was at once commanding and reassuring.

She seemed much smaller in the studio than she did behind the footlights on a stage. Just under five foot three, she had a long torso and relatively short, muscular legs. Her black hair was tied back with a ribbon, and her deep-set eyes took in everything.

Following the floor exercises, Martha had the students stand up to perform balancing exercises and to lift their legs at the barre. After that she had them move across the studio floor, walking, running, skipping, and leaping. Finally they began to work on new steps and movements that Martha was trying out.

Her experiments with movement were giving birth to a new dance technique, a way of moving that was uniquely hers. Working with her own body, and with the bodies of her dancers, she was seeking to convey, through dance, unspoken needs, desires, and dreams, and universal emotions such as joy or jealousy or grief. "Dance is another way of putting things," she said. "If it could be said in words, it would be; but outside of words, outside of painting, outside of sculpture, *inside* the body is an interior landscape which is revealed in movement."

The dance movements that Graham invented were very different from the graceful illusions of classical ballet. Ballet is an aerial art; ballerinas make a spectacle of defying gravity, as though they are lighter than air. Graham's dancers reveled in the downward pull of gravity; instead of dancing on their toes, they hugged the ground in bare feet. Ballet seeks to appear effortless, to make everything look easy. Graham wanted to reveal effort, in the belief that life itself involves effort. Ballet, with its rounded arms and smooth flowing lines, is graceful and elegant, while Graham's modern dance was spare, stark, and angular, stripped of inessentials and filled with tension.

"My quarrel was never with ballet itself," she said many years later, "but that, as used in classical ballets, it did not say enough, especially when it came to intense drama, to passion. It was that very lack that sent me into the kind of work I do, so that I could get beyond the surface and to that inner world."

To help reveal that "inner world" of emotions and dreams, Graham started from a fundamental fact of life: the act of breathing. She noted that changes in breathing—a gasp, a sigh, a sob, a laugh—suggest deep-seated emotional states. By observing the body's changes as a person breathes, she developed the principles of "contraction" and "release" and built a whole vocabulary of movements upon them.

In a contraction, her dancers drew their torsos into a gut-clenching grip, tightening, or contracting, the stomach muscles and pushing the pelvis forward. In a release, their bodies returned to a normal state. The action that triggered the contraction and release of muscles was breathing. Squeezing out the breath was a contraction. Taking in the breath was a release.

Squeezing out the breath was a contraction.
Photograph by Barbara Morgan.

A contraction started in the gut and could attain whiplash intensity as it radiated out to the arms, legs, and head in a jerking, or percussive, motion. A forceful contraction could send the dancer's body from a standing position right down to the floor. It could jerk the body into a turn, or thrust it into a leap.

By controlling breathing in this way, Graham felt she could convey heightened emotions. Intense feelings were revealed not simply by gestures of the hands and arms, but through powerful contractions and releases originating in the muscles of the torso. She regarded the torso—the site of the lungs, the heart, and the spine—as the vital center of a dancer's energy. Every emotion, she believed, starts or is visible first in the torso.

Along with the controlled use of contraction and release, Graham and her dancers embraced the power of gravity. Frequently her dance movements took her down to the floor. She invented a series of falls in which the dancer, on bent knees, sinks slowly backward in a spiral motion, with nothing to break the fall, then recovers by reversing the process and spiraling forward and upward to stand erect. The knees were used like hinges to lower then raise the body, and the stage floor became part of the dance movement. Graham's falls, according to Agnes de Mille, were "not so much a crashing down as a dissolving, a melting and sliding, a communion with the ground and then a recovery."

"The floor is a direction," said Graham. While expressing sadness or

Graham's dance movements also took her down to the floor. Photograph by Barbara Morgan.

despair, she did not simply bow her head or clasp her hands to her chest. She allowed her entire body to sink downward. "When you are very upset," she said, "you have a sinking feeling inside you. So as a dancer I showed on the *outside* what was happening on the *inside*—my whole body sank or fell to the floor."

Graham was constantly expanding her dance vocabulary as she discovered meaningful and dramatic ways of moving. Her dancers' earthbound walk and scampering run, their jetlike leaps and rebounding falls, the throbbing tension and surging energy of her early dances, were meant to ignite the viewer's imagination, to reveal inner conflicts and passions, the "interior landscape" that we all share.

Classical ballet masters compose in an inherited dance language that has been handed down for generations. Graham was inventing her own vocabulary of movements, an entirely new language of dance. She was creating a body of work that was hers alone and no one else's.

Along with her radically new dance style Graham was pioneering a new approach to the music that accompanied her dances. In 1928 Louis Horst set a precedent by composing the music for *Fragments* after Graham had created the dance, reversing the usual practice in which a dance was matched to already composed music. "That was the first dance music that we know of in America that was done *to* the dance," said Horst. Over the years he introduced Martha to the work of many prominent contemporary composers, such as Aaron Copland, Samuel Barber, and Gian Carlo Menotti, who collaborated with her by composing original music set to her dances.

Costumes and makeup were another area of experimentation. In her early work Graham favored simple, unadorned costumes so that the dancers' movements could be seen without the distractions of scarves, veils, jewels, and other trappings. White makeup made their faces look like masks, with each mouth a gash of Kandinskian red. Often the women wore long tube-shaped dresses of wool jersey or other fabrics that stretched and folded as the body moved. Later, Graham would jokingly refer to the late 1920s and early 1930s as "my period of long woolens."

"My period of long woolens." Graham in *Ekstasis*, 1933.
Photograph by Soichi Sunami.

She designed the costumes herself, buying the material at discount shops. Her budget was a dollar a dress. The outfits were sewn by the dancers, who sat cross-legged on the studio floor, dresses spread across their knees, working together as in a sewing bee or church social. "Of course, when we all sat on the floor and sewed those darn things out of wool jersey, she'd turn into a different person," Bessie Schonberg remembered. "She told very entertaining stories—she turned into your Aunt Jane dishing up stories."

Of all her early dances, the most haunting was a 1930 solo called *Lamentation*. As if to dramatize her ideas about movement, Martha performed the dance while seated on a low bench. Dressed in a tubelike shroud of stretch jersey, her head hooded, with only her face, hands, and bare feet showing, she sat with her knees spread widely to either side, her hands clenched together between them.

As the somber notes of Zoltán Kodály's music began, this mummylike figure began to rock with anguish from side to side, plunging her hands deep into the stretching fabric, writhing and twisting as if trying to break out of her shroud, a figure of unbearable sorrow and grief. And as her body moved, so did the stretch jersey of the costume she wore, folding in upon itself, forming frightening contours and shadows. She did not dance *about* grief, she said, but sought "the thing itself"—the very embodiment of grief.

People who saw Martha Graham perform this dance would never forget it. After one performance a woman in the audience asked to see Martha backstage. Weeping bitterly, she explained that her nine-year-old son had been struck and killed by a car several months earlier. She had been unable to express her grief and surrender to tears until the evening she saw *Lamentation.* "You will never know what you have done for me tonight," she said. "Thank you." Sobbing in relief, she mourned in Martha's arms.

"What I learned that night," Graham wrote, "is that there is always one person in the audience to whom you speak."

The embodiment of grief: *Lamentation,* 1930. Photograph by Soichi Sunami.

Martha Graham in "Hymn to the Virgin" from *Primitive Mysteries*, surrounded by
Anna Sokolow, Lily Mehlman, unidentified, and Freema Nadler, 1931.
Photograph by Edward Moeller.

CHAPTER SIX

TESTING THE $\mathcal{L}$IMITS

MARTHA PUT IN MANY HOURS of teaching every day. Her students worked on the demanding stretching, bending, and breathing exercises that they called "the torture," becoming supple and muscular in the process. They were made aware of the pelvis and the power of the spine, which Graham called "the tree of life."

An important part of the training was a snakelike spiral movement, in which a student coiled and uncoiled on the floor, giving strength and flexibility to the spine. "Now, let's see you do that exercise as if you *needed* to do it!" Martha would say.

To help her students visualize the movements she was after, she came up with some striking images. When arching backward, students were told to "think of Joan of Arc resisting a sword that is piercing her chest." A certain kick of the leg was like "a horse rearing up." A long, slow backward fall was like letting "a gentle waterfall flow down the body." Graham told her students to walk across the room as if their hearts were on the wall.

The movements she devised were based on her own body, on what she herself was able to do. With her unusual build, her strength and flexibility, she could do plenty. Her legs were short and muscular compared to the long, slender legs of most dancers. She had powerful thighs, and she could kick a leg straight upward in a split of 180 degrees.

Between classes she would shut the studio door and work by herself. A red ribbon tied to the doorknob was a warning that she must not be disturbed. "Movement in modern dance is the product not of invention but of discovery—discovery of what the body will do," she said.

She made exorbitant demands on herself and her students, terrifying many and alienating some. But most students admired her, and the dedicated young women who danced as members of the Group came to worship her. "Everybody was hypnotized, absolutely magnetized by Martha," Dorothy Bird recalled. "She opened our eyes to the arts. I was on fire."

Portrait of Martha Graham, around 1930. Photograph by Soichi Sunami.

Martha seemed to live in a realm apart. To be with her in the studio or on the stage was to share her magic, to be part of the creative act. When she stood in front of the class, small and straight, her eyes blazing and her feet gripping the floor, and said, "Wherever a dancer stands ready, that spot is holy ground," she held out a vision that her students found hard to resist.

Over the years her Dance Group was like a family, celebrating birthdays and anniversaries, throwing a big party every Christmas. On those occasions husbands and boyfriends were admitted to the studio. Everyone brought food and wine, Louis played the piano, Martha told jokes, and they all sang and danced and had a wonderful time.

Martha shared a close bond with her dancers, but she took care to stay out of their personal affairs. The life she led left little time for relationships outside the studio, and in any case she knew that emotional entanglements could destroy a dance company's discipline. If she seemed distant or aloof, her dancers did not blame her. They felt privileged and proud to be her instruments, and they gave themselves completely, willingly. They knew that Martha did indeed care about them, that she would respond to a personal crisis with genuine warmth and concern.

During the 1930s, when her company was on tour, one of the dancers received a telegram with news that her father had died. Martha asked the girl to come to her hotel room. When she arrived, Martha drew her gently over to the sofa. "Sit down with me, here," she said. As the dancer began to speak of her father and weep, Martha gathered her up in her arms, shifted her to her own lap, and rocked her tenderly like a baby as she shared the young girl's grief.

Martha's personal life centered on Louis—her beloved Luigi, as she called him. She worked with him, relied on his advice, and took pride in his independent achievements as a composer, teacher, and dance critic. Though they lived apart, they spent practically every day together. They were as close as a couple can be, and yet their friends were aware of an unspoken tension in their relationship.

Louis was rumpled and heavyset, but he had great charm. Many young women found him fascinating and wanted to please him, and he in turn

Enjoying a quiet moment with Louis Horst and Socrates.

enjoyed and often invited their attentions. And while he had long been separated from his wife, Betty, who lived in San Francisco, he continued to support her and would not ask for a divorce. Even so, he clearly adored Martha.

Martha never expressed a yearning for a conventional domestic life. A vine-covered cottage by a babbling brook just wasn't for her. She was devoted to her work, totally absorbed in what she was doing. As everyone knew, she would allow nothing to stand in her way. And though she rarely confided in anyone about her affair with Louis, some of her friends suspected that she wanted him to marry her, and that she felt deeply wounded when he hesitated and delayed.

Martha would never admit this. Years later, she claimed that she wasn't really in love with Louis. "He became my lover, yes, but it was like loving a child, because I was a child," she said. "But I was never in love with him. I was deeply fond of him and I believed in his word."

True love or not, Martha depended on Louis in a thousand different ways. He was her most loyal supporter and her toughest critic, bluntly honest in his comments.

"Why *that* movement?" he would demand gruffly. "That's not good enough. Can't you find something better?"

"But Louis, you're destroying the idea," Martha would complain. "You're killing my inspiration!"

"If the inspiration is that weak," he would growl, "believe me, you can afford to get rid of it and get busy on something else!"

"You're putting out the fire," she accused him once, bristling at his sharp criticism.

"Only to make a bigger one," he replied.

Martha's standards for herself were even stricter than Louis's. Never satisfied, she would agonize over last-minute changes and decisions. Louis had to push her to finish new dances and get them ready for the stage.

As the time for a performance approached, an atmosphere of crisis took hold. Martha might decide that the costumes, which she had designed herself, were all wrong. In a frenzy, she would rip them apart, put her dancers to work with needles and thread, and remake the costumes until they suited her. When there wasn't time to finish resewing, the dancers went onstage with the costumes held together by safety pins. They felt that this kind of tension helped keep Martha's creative energy at a high pitch.

Throughout the late 1920s and early 1930s, Graham continued to experiment with new movements, new dances, and new themes. An evening with Martha Graham and her Dance Group was always a demanding and unpredictable experience. Yet Martha had a following now, and her concerts often commanded full houses. Critic John Martin praised her as the most gifted dancer of her generation. "No other dancer has yet touched the borders to which she has extended the compass of movement," he wrote. "She has proved the body capable of a phenomenal range."

Not everyone was that enthusiastic. Some critics and concertgoers continued to find Graham's dances ugly and obscure. "Innocent people who were introduced to modern dance by Martha in her sledgehammer, unsmiling, angular period sometimes said to themselves, 'If this is modern dance, no more!'" wrote critic Walter Terry.

Martha wanted audiences to respond to her work, but she was willing to take risks, eager to push her talent to the limit. As a creative artist she was never content simply to repeat herself.

Her work was influenced deeply by a trip she took with Louis in the summer of 1930, when they spent several weeks visiting Native American communities in New Mexico. Martha was fascinated by the southwestern landscape of mountain, desert, and sky, by the blending of Indian, Christian, and Spanish cultures, and by the people's deeply felt religious practices and ceremonial dances. When she returned to New York, she began a new work called *Primitive Mysteries*, inspired by a solemn Indian-Hispanic ritual honoring the Virgin Mary.

She worked on *Primitive Mysteries* with her dancers for over a year before she felt that the piece was ready to perform. At the last minute, however, she was assailed by doubts and misgivings. The dance just wasn't working, she complained. It was a failure. During a dress rehearsal the night before the premiere, she was so anxious and dissatisfied that her nerves snapped.

Shaking with frustration, she ordered the dancers to pack up and go home. She was going to take the new dance off the program. It wasn't ready. It wasn't good enough. "That's enough!" she screamed. "Get out of my sight! Go home! Go away!" Then she stomped off the stage and locked herself in her dressing room.

Louis, always sensible during one of Martha's crises, calmed the dancers down. Quietly, he told them to stay. After a while Martha's mood lifted and she returned to the stage. She didn't seem in the least surprised that everyone was still there, waiting. Without a word the dancers went back to work, rehearsing the dance that would be acclaimed a masterpiece.

Primitive Mysteries was performed for the first time on February 2, 1931, at the Craig Theater in New York. Dressed entirely in white, Graham danced against a background chorus of twelve women wearing dark blue. Horst's score for flute, oboe, and piano hinted at Native American melodies, while the dance itself, stark, simple, and intense, captured with gathering force the exaltation of an ancient religious ceremony.

Critics hailed *Primitive Mysteries* as Graham's most compelling work so far. "The most significant choreography which has yet come out of Amer-

(right) Study for *Primitive Mysteries*. Photograph by Soichi Sunami.

(below) Inspired by Native American religious rites, *Primitive Mysteries* was acclaimed as Graham's first true masterpiece. Photograph by Barbara Morgan.

ica . . . it achieves a mood which actually lifts both spectators and dancers to the rarefied heights of spiritual ecstasy," wrote Mary F. Watkins of the *New York Herald-Tribune*.

The dance was a hit with audiences too. At the premiere, the cheering crowd gave Martha and her dancers twenty-three curtain calls. And this was the work that she had almost thrown onto the scrap heap.

Never content, Martha was constantly testing herself. In dances like *Four Insincerities* and *Moment Rustica* (both 1929), she revealed a talent for parody and comedy. In 1930 she displayed the virtuosity of a prima ballerina when she danced the role of The Chosen One in Igor Stravinsky's *Rite of Spring*, under the direction of the famed classical ballet choreographer Léonide Massine. And during the Christmas holidays in 1932 Martha and her Group performed in the gala opening program of New York's lavish new theater, Radio City Music Hall, as Louis Horst conducted the orchestra.

That year Graham became the first dancer to win a Guggenheim Fellowship, an award that usually went to distinguished American writers, musicians, or painters. Always on the lookout for new horizons, she used the grant money to travel with Louis to Mexico, where they explored Aztec and Mayan archeological sites and witnessed ancient tribal dances.

One day they climbed to the top of the sacred Pyramid of the Sun at Teotihuacán, near Mexico City. "It was so striking going up those steps and arriving at the top to be absorbed in a very hallowed place," Martha wrote. "I raised my hands high above my head and was enthralled by the wind and the sun. . . . "

Climbing the Pyramid of the Sun in Mexico, 1932.

Martha Graham in "Satyric Festival Song" from *Dance Songs*, 1932.
Photograph by Barbara Morgan.

CHAPTER SEVEN

NEW *F*RONTIERS

BEGINNING IN 1934 MARTHA and Louis spent their summers at Bennington College in southern Vermont, "a wonderful place where we were given the freedom and possibility to make our dances." Bennington's newly founded School of the Dance was headed by Martha Hill, a former member of Graham's Dance Group. Hill invited America's leading modern dancers to visit the campus each summer, to conduct workshops and create new works for performance at the school's annual festival of contemporary dance.

Dancers, aspiring dancers, and dance teachers flocked to Bennington from all over the country, eager for a chance to work with the best-known figures in the field. The faculty included the so-called "Big Four" of modern dance—Martha Graham, Doris Humphrey, Charles Weidman, and Hanya Holm—along with composers, stage designers, poets, dance critics, and others who came together on the tree-shaded campus to form a vital creative community.

Louis and Martha would arrive on campus in their sputtering old Model-T Ford, an open car piled high with luggage. Sitting at the wheel was the dancer Bonnie Bird, since neither Martha nor Louis knew how to drive. "Up the winding road, under the leafy elms, the car would noisily chug its way until its royal occupants were in full campus view," wrote Graham's biographer Ernestine Stodell. "Martha and Louis in the back seat,

Martha and Louis
arrive at
Bennington College.

scarves and neckties flying, hats shielding faces from sun and wind, and in
their arms, held protectively, [Martha's] dachshunds Allah and Mädel.

"Was it Martha's sense of theater that made everything she did seem
spectacular? Whatever it was . . . the sight of Martha Graham always created a stir."

Bennington's summer dance program offered a wonderful opportunity
to develop new work away from the financial pressures of the New York theater scene. In 1934 the United States was struggling to emerge from the
Great Depression. Times were hard and money was scarce. Bennington pro-
vided rent-free rehearsal studios, a well-equipped workshop where sets could
be made, a theater for performances, and a chance for the pioneers of modern dance to exchange ideas.

Martha had already created a distinctive new way of dancing. She had
won critical acclaim and a growing audience, but she continued to take creative risks, striking out in new and unexpected directions.

All along she had been striving to create a "uniquely American" style of dance. "The American dancer owes a duty to the American audience," she said. "We must look to America to bring forth an art as powerful as the country itself." During the 1930s she began to explore some of the forces that have shaped American culture, expressing through dance what it was like to be an American and what America meant to her.

Martha's ancestors had pressed into the wilderness with axe and saw, putting down roots in what was then the American frontier. She celebrated that pioneer spirit in 1935 with a groundbreaking solo called *Frontier.* It had an original score by Louis Horst, and, for the first time, a set. Until then Martha had danced on a bare stage.

Graham dances in front of Isamu Noguchi's innovative stage set for *Frontier,* 1935.
Photograph by Barbara Morgan.

Frontier. . . . leaping joyously through space with head-high, sideways kicks.
Photograph by Barbara Morgan.

For the set she turned not to a scene painter but to a young American sculptor, Isamu Noguchi. The set he designed for *Frontier* was deceptively simple. Instead of the two-dimensional painted backdrops and side panels traditionally used in theatrical dance performances, Noguchi built a three-dimensional set that stood on the stage floor like a piece of sculpture. Two horizontal poles at the center of the stage suggested the wooden bars of a rail fence at a frontier outpost. Behind this fence two ropes stretched upward and outward from the floor to the unknown reaches above and beyond, suggesting the boundless plains of the American West.

As the dance opened, Martha was seen leaning against this fence with one foot planted firmly on the ground, the other lifted and placed high on the top fence rail. Dressed in a pioneer woman's homespun jumper, she began by rotating her torso, and as her head turned to scan the horizon, she broke out into a broad smile. For the first time she discarded the masklike facial expression that had been a hallmark of her earlier dances.

"I was there," wrote Walter Terry, "and it was the most ravishing smile I have ever seen in my life. In that smile was mirrored the promise that a frontierswoman saw as she looked over a vast new land. . . . With that smile, Martha Graham invited us to step forward into a new dance experience that would change the course of theater for decades, perhaps centuries, to come."

Noguchi's simple fence became an essential part of the dance as Martha moved about the stage—advancing toward the audience with bold, out-flung gestures, pacing off the land with simple, measured steps, leaping joyously through space with head-high sideways kicks, then returning to rest triumphantly against the fence. In a solo lasting just six and a half minutes, she conveyed a wide range of feelings—loneliness, wonder, courage, determination, optimism, joy—and evoked the spirit of westward-moving pioneers.

The stage set for *Frontier* was Noguchi's first. Martha had met him during the late 1920s, when his sister was a member of her dance group, and he was to be a lifelong friend and collaborator. He worked with Martha for more than fifty years, winning recognition as both a brilliant sculptor and an innovative stage designer.

Frontier became Martha Graham's trademark, her most popular solo. She performed the dance again and again with great success as she traveled across the country on her company's first transcontinental tour. But she was still her own toughest critic. After a performance in Oakland, California, that had been cheered by an admiring audience, a friend asked, "What's the matter, Martha? You seem depressed."

"I am," Martha replied. "It was a terrible performance. I've never danced so badly in my life."

She was never satisfied, never truly at rest. The more successful she became, the harder she drove her dancers and herself.

While she was hard on herself, she did not always take kindly to criticism from others. Once, when an unfavorable review by John Martin

Lunch at Bennington College: Erick Hawkins, Doris Humphrey, Charles Weidman, Martha Graham, and Louis Horst, 1941.

appeared in *The New York Times*, Martha angrily confronted him in the faculty dining room at Bennington. Livid, she gave Martin a blistering tongue-lashing, spitting out her words as everyone else in the room averted their eyes and shifted uneasily in their seats. Until that morning Martin and Graham had been warm personal friends. While he continued to respect Martha and praise her work, they were never close again.

"She is a genius," Martin told Agnes de Mille. "She will do what she wants to do and what she feels she needs to do, and she doesn't really give a damn about anybody else or about friendships. That's what one must expect of a genius."

Martha's explosive temperament, her unpredictable moods, both baffled and thrilled everyone around her. If something went wrong in the studio or during a rehearsal, her angry outbursts left no one untouched. Yet she could be a winning companion, mischievous, sly, merry, with a wicked sense of humor. "She was great fun to be with," said de Mille. "She had an enormous sense of fun."

De Mille owned an old jalopy, a convertible with a hole in its canvas roof. On rainy evenings Martha would poke her umbrella up through the hole and open it above the car, and the two of them would drive up Fifth Avenue on their way to a concert "giggling, elegant, and dry."

By now Graham's reputation had spread far beyond the New York dance world. Students came from all over the United States and Canada to attend her classes at Bennington and in Greenwich Village. With Louis and her dancers she toured the country regularly. And she collaborated on dramatic Broadway stage productions with actress Katharine Cornell, poet-playwright Archibald MacLeish, and other well-known theater personalities.

In 1937 Graham became the first American dancer ever invited to perform at the White House. The invitation came from Eleanor Roosevelt, the president's wife. When Martha and Louis arrived, they were invited to have an informal dinner with the president's family and a few guests before the performance, but Martha declined. "She didn't come in to dinner because she wanted to make up, and she was too nervous to eat," Louis recalled. He joined the presidential dinner party without her.

Afterward Martha danced *Frontier* and three other solos in the East Ballroom as Louis played the piano. When the performance ended, Mrs. Roosevelt announced, "This poor girl hasn't had any dinner. Come along!" The first lady led Martha into the White House kitchen, found some left-over roast beef, sliced it herself, and chatted amiably with her guest as Martha gratefully ate.

Mrs. Roosevelt wanted Martha and Louis to spend the night, but no, Martha insisted on catching the midnight train back to New York in order to conduct rehearsals the next day. "That's too bad," said Mrs. Roosevelt. "Maybe another time." Then she embraced Martha and thanked her. "How kind of you to come," the first lady said. "How very kind to have made the effort to come."

A year earlier Martha had turned down an invitation from the government of Nazi Germany to perform at the International Dance Festival, part

Graham expressed her anguish over the brutal Spanish Civil War in *Deep Song*, 1937. Photograph by Barbara Morgan.

of the 1936 Olympic Games being held in Berlin. By representing the United States at the festival, she would have gained worldwide publicity and the prospect of substantial financial support. She refused. "It never entered my mind even for a second to say yes," she said. "How could I dance in Nazi Germany?"

Martha knew that the Nazis were already persecuting Jews and other minorities. She wrote to Joseph Goebbels, the German propaganda minister: "I would find it impossible to dance in Germany at the present time. So many artists whom I respect and admire have been persecuted, have been deprived of the right to work for ridiculous and unsatisfactory reasons, that I should consider it impossible to identify myself, by accepting your invitation, with the regime that has made such things possible. In addition, some of my concert group would not be welcomed in Germany."

Several members of her group were Jewish. German authorities insisted that all of Graham's dancers would be treated with courtesy, but she would have nothing to do with it. "Do you think I would ask them to go?" she replied. She refused to associate herself with the Nazi regime in any way, setting an example. No American dance company agreed to perform at the Olympic festival that year.

After World War II Martha learned that her name had been placed on a list of those to be "taken care of" when the Nazis controlled the United States. "I took it as a great compliment," she said.

Erick Hawkins. Photograph by Barbara Morgan.

CHAPTER EIGHT

ENTER ERICK

DURING THE 1930s MARTHA GRAHAM created nearly fifty new dances. At the top of her form now, she was constantly exploring new ways to speak to people through dance. Then she astonished everyone in the dance world by adding something else that was new—*men!*

Erick Hawkins joined Graham's company in 1938, followed by Merce Cunningham a year later. The introduction of male dancers to the company had a dramatic impact on Martha's creative work, and on her personal life.

Hawkins, a native of Trinidad, Colorado, had been trained in classical ballet. Martha saw him dance for the first time when he appeared at Bennington with Ballet Caravan, a small company founded by Lincoln Kirstein, who later became co-founder and general director of the New York City Ballet. After watching Hawkins perform, Martha went backstage and singled out the handsome young man for praise.

Soon afterward Hawkins began to attend classes at Martha's Greenwich Village studio, and then at Bennington. She asked him to teach her students some basic ballet movements. Erick, in turn, asked Martha to use him in some modest capacity in her company, if only as a walk-on. During the summer of 1938 Martha decided to give Erick a leading role in her new dance, *American Document*. He became the company's first male dancer.

American Document was the most theatrical production Graham had ever attempted. A panoramic view of American history presented in the form of a minstrel show, the work featured familiar folk rhythms, colorful costumes, and readings from famous American texts. Hawkins, tall and muscular, with rugged good looks, dominated the stage as the male lead. He danced three love duets with Graham and one solo. The cast also included a second man, a narrator, who spoke lines from the Declaration of Independence, Abraham Lincoln's Gettysburg Address, Walt Whitman's poetry, the Bible, and other significant documents.

Spoken words—a device that Graham would use again in some of her future works—helped make *American Document* easily understood and popular with a wide and responsive audience. At the same time male-female duets introduced an electrifying new emotional dimension to Graham's

Martha Graham and Erick Hawkins in "Puritan Love Duet" from *American Document*, 1938. Photograph by Barbara Morgan.

work. Now she could explore love, jealousy, and sexual passion in her dances.

"My being a man let Martha be a woman, and in that role her dancing changed," Hawkins said later. "She came into her own as a woman, and she had someone like myself to take the other side of passion."

Erick's entrance into the company broke new ground but did not come without cost. Martha had named him a principal dancer, the only soloist besides herself, pushing him ahead of veteran dancers who had been dedicated members of the company for years. Louis was against the whole idea. He wanted the company to remain entirely female. And many of the dancers resented Erick's favored treatment. Behind his back they called him "the torso." When Martha began to ask Erick's opinions and invite his criticisms, she was faced with an open rebellion. Four of her best women dancers left the company.

It wasn't easy to sever ties with Martha. With her single-minded intensity she exerted an almost hypnotic power over her dancers' lives. While she was demanding, she was also loyal to her dancers, and when they left the company, they sometimes felt that they were abandoning her personally. They would tear themselves away only after agonized hesitation and indecision.

Merce Cunningham joined the company as its second male dancer in 1939. A spectacularly talented young man from Centralia, Washington, he turned out to be one of Graham's greatest discoveries. He was barely twenty years old when Martha tapped him for a leading role in her first major comic work, *Every Soul Is a Circus*. She had touched upon humor and satire before, but in *Circus* she veered wildly into comedy, showing that she could poke fun at herself and at the foibles of others.

Graham danced the role of the Empress of the Arena, a vain, scatterbrained star performer who is "her own most appreciative spectator." She flirts shamelessly with her dream lover, an Acrobat, danced by Cunningham, who sweeps her off her feet with his aerial antics. But she is "tamed" by her lord and master, a stern and pompous Ringmaster, danced by Hawkins, who keeps her at whip's end. At the end the two men grow tired

Merce Cunningham, Martha Graham, and Erick Hawkins in *Every Soul Is a Circus*, 1939. Photograph by Barbara Morgan.

of the Empress's frivolous flirtations and walk off the stage, leaving her bewildered and alone.

With works like *American Document* and *Every Soul Is a Circus*, Graham was entering a new phase of her career—what would soon become known as "The Theater of Martha Graham." She was broadening her repertoire, expanding the range of moods and emotions that her dances expressed, and shifting to a warmer, freer, more lyrical dance style. In the future she would turn more and more to large-scale theatrical productions that combined dance, music, costumes, and sets, and, increasingly, humor, satire, and high drama.

Looking back at her earlier dances, she said: "I'm afraid that I used to hit audiences over the head with a sledgehammer because I was so determined that they see and feel what I was trying to do. Now I know...that you must draw people to you, like a magnet—perhaps by the intensity of your own belief.

"Now that we modern dancers have left our period of 'long woolens' behind us, we must prove to our audiences that our theater pieces can have color, warmth, and entertainment value. We must convince our audiences that we belong in the American theater."

As Empress of the Arena in *Every Soul Is a Circus*, Graham displayed a gift for humor and satire. Photograph by Barbara Morgan.

By 1940 Graham's company was made up of nine women and five men. That year Erick Hawkins and Merce Cunningham were both featured in *Letter to the World*, Martha's first true dance-drama, complete with acts and scenes like a play. Once again she broke new ground, creating through dance, music, and spoken words a moving biographical portrait of Emily Dickinson, the reclusive New England poet.

There is a legend that Dickinson fell in love with a married minister, whom she saw once or twice and might have run away with. True or not, it is a fact that she never married and lived most of her life in the seclusion of her father's house. Feeling that love was forbidden to her, she expressed her

Martha Graham as Emily Dickinson (The One Who Dances) greets Merce Cunningham as March, the spirit of Spring, in *Letter to the World*, 1940. Photograph by Barbara Morgan.

emotions and intense religious yearnings through her poems, most of which were unpublished in her lifetime. According to Graham's program notes, "out of the tragedy of her loss will be born the poet."

To show different sides of Dickinson's personality, Graham created two "Emilys," portrayed by two dancers. The One Who Speaks, played in the New York premiere by dancer Jean Erdman, moves across the stage with dignified and measured steps and speaks lines from Dickinson's poems. She represents the Emily known to the world as a polite and proper spinster. The One Who Dances, played by Graham, represents Dickinson's hidden emotional life, her passionate, yearning, romantic self, what Graham called a person's "inner landscape."

Other characters suggest different facets of Dickinson's personality at various times in her life. Hawkins portrayed the mysterious Dark Beloved, a fleeting romantic presence who symbolizes the power and attraction of the outside world. Cunningham was cast as March, the frolicsome, wayward spirit of Spring. And Jane Dudley played the stern and austere Ancestress, representing Dickinson's ever-watchful New England conscience.

Letter to the World does not unfold in a straightforward chronological manner. Like a movie or a dream, the dance uses flashbacks, skipping back and forth in time. It also moves back and forth between Dickinson's inner and outer lives, as represented by different dancers. These narrative techniques were new to dance, and when the work was first performed at Bennington in the summer of 1940, it mystified many of those who saw it. "Better let it sleep in the Vermont hills," wrote John Martin.

Graham herself wasn't satisfied. She went back to work on the piece and made many changes, clarifying and simplifying, while Hunter Johnson, the composer, reshaped the score. When the revised version of *Letter to the World* was finally presented in New York, the work was pronounced a great success, "one of the most beautiful creations yet to be revealed in American dance," according to John Martin, whose opinion had changed. "It is not only the greatest achievement so far in the career of one of the most distinguished artists of our time, but it opens up new territory for the dance."

"Sometimes a dance takes two years, two years of brooding, of think-

Letter to the World: The One Who Dances. Photograph by Barbara Morgan.

ing," Graham said long afterward. "You put it away, you forget about it. It comes back. It was that way with *Letter to the World*."

Early in Martha's career, when she was struggling for recognition, many of her dances dealt with the plight of the outsider, the lonely rebel, the social outcast. Gradually the themes of her dances changed, reflecting her interests and concerns at the time. Since meeting Erick, Martha had been thinking, above all, about the bewildering complexities of personal relationships and the role they play in an artist's life.

In *Letter to the World* Emily Dickinson is portrayed as a solitary figure who sacrifices a personal life, embraces her destiny as a poet, and devotes herself totally to her art. As the dance ends, The One Who Speaks sits quietly alone on her garden bench, half turned from the audience, reconciled to her fate, and repeats Dickinson's lines:

> This is my letter to the World
> That never wrote to Me.

Recognized today as a masterpiece, *Letter to the World* explores a theme that concerned Martha deeply—that of the dedicated artist who is destined to live, dream, and work alone, forever an outsider to the kind of happiness enjoyed by most people. Was that to be Martha's destiny?

At Bennington Martha had become close friends with the writer Joseph Campbell. He asked her once if she could ever commit herself fully to love. "If I were to take that step," Martha told him, "I would lose my art."

Erick Hawkins and Martha Graham during an outdoor rehearsal at Bennington College in the summer of 1939. Photographs by Barbara Morgan.

CHAPTER NINE

A LOVE LETTER

MARTHA WAS APPROACHING the age of fifty, but her powers as a performer were as great as ever. She created one impressive work after another, toured widely with her company, taught at colleges and dance schools around the country, and held private classes at her New York studio.

She no longer lived and worked in the same place. She had moved to a new and larger studio at 66 Fifth Avenue, in Greenwich Village, and rented an apartment around the corner—two rooms on the top floor of a brownstone that she tried to keep separate from her daily routine of classes and rehearsals.

Erick had become an important member of her company. He often conducted rehearsals, leaving Martha free to work on new dances. He took over the physical management of the productions, supervising the setting up, dismantling, and shipping of scenery and sets. He suggested new ideas and helped raise funds from private donors to finance Martha's ambitious theatrical projects.

Erick made himself indispensable. More and more, Martha depended on him. She still worked closely with Louis, "but emotionally we had drifted apart," Horst recalled. Louis was still married. Erick was young, single, and clearly interested in Martha. It was plain to everyone in the company that she was seriously infatuated with him.

On December 7, 1941, Martha and her dancers were touring the South on their way to an engagement in Cuba when they learned that Japanese war planes had just bombed the American naval base at Pearl Harbor, Hawaii. The next day, at a little beachfront cafe in Miami, Florida, they huddled around a radio and heard President Franklin D. Roosevelt ask Congress to declare a state of war.

That night they boarded their ship bound for Havana, Cuba. Martha had never learned to swim and she was terrified of the water, a fear compounded now by her terror of torpedoes. Germany was about to enter the war as an ally of Japan, and rumors were flying that hostile German submarines were lurking nearby. "I remember speaking with some of the sailors about how one never knew where the submarines might be, and they said, 'Oh, in the west [the Pacific], not here,'" dancer and choreographer Sophie Maslow remembered. "Of course, later we found out there were German submarines in those very waters. But we went to Cuba, and when we got there we were greeted with great joy."

They returned home safely, arriving in New York to find the country mobilizing for World War II. Graham lost several of her male dancers to the wartime draft (Hawkins was rejected because of poor eyesight), but she kept in touch with them, writing long, chatty letters to members of her company who were serving overseas. To David Zellmer, now an Army Air Corps pilot in the Pacific, she wrote: "I wish I could say all the things that buzz around in my heart about you and your safety, which I never seem to forget for an instant."

During the war years Martha met Bethsabee de Rothschild, a member of the wealthy European banking family. Rothschild, who was Jewish, had escaped from France in 1940, just ahead of the invading Nazi armies. After settling in New York, she took a dance class at Graham's Fifth Avenue studio. While she had little talent as a dancer, she fell wholeheartedly in love with Martha Graham's artistic vision.

A shy, unassuming woman with a slight lisp, Bethsabee attended every Graham performance and began to tour with the company at her own expense, volunteering to help out in any way that she could. She became

Punch and the Judy, 1941: From left to right, Jean Erdman, Ethel Butler, Merce Cunningham, Jane Dudley, Erick Hawkins, Martha Graham, David Zellmer, Nina Fonaroff, Pearl Lang, Mark Ryder, David Campbell.

Martha's generous patron and loyal friend, paying the company's deficits at the end of each season and helping to underwrite the costs of new productions.

Another wartime friendship that meant a great deal to Martha was with Helen Keller, the noted blind and deaf author, lecturer, and crusader for the handicapped. Keller would visit Martha's studio and "watch" the dancing by feeling the vibrations of the dancers' feet on the wooden floor. Once she asked Martha to describe jumping to her. "What is jumping?" she asked. "I don't understand."

Martha asked Merce Cunningham to demonstrate. She placed Helen's hands on Merce's waist as everyone in the studio looked on. When Merce

Helen Keller visits Graham's studio in the early 1940s.

jumped into the air, Helen's hands rose and fell with his body. Her face lit up with a joyous smile. She threw up her arms and exclaimed, "How like thought! How like the mind it is!"

"She was a great lady, and very funny too," Martha wrote. "She was, perhaps, the most gallant woman I have ever known."

In 1943 Graham completed a brooding new work called *Deaths and Entrances* (music by Hunter Johnson), another psychological portrait in music and dance. This time she probed the somber lives and turbulent passions of the Brontë sisters, Emily, Charlotte, and Anne, the nineteenth-century English authors famous for their novels of high romance: *Wuthering Heights* (Emily), *Jane Eyre* (Charlotte), and *The Tenant of Wildfell Hall* (Anne).

Graham danced the role of Emily, who looks back at her life through the telescopic lens of memory, while the dancers around her symbolize the secret inner world of her loves, desires, and fears. Emily appears to be facing an urgent emotional choice: She must choose between the Dark Beloved, danced by Erick Hawkins, and the Poetic Beloved, played by Merce Cunningham. In the end she chooses neither, selecting instead a mysterious glass goblet that seems to symbolize her artistic calling.

Erick Hawkins as the Dark Beloved, Martha Graham as Emily Brontë, and Merce Cunningham as the Poetic Beloved in *Deaths and Entrances*, 1943. Photograph by Barbara Morgan.

Like many of Graham's works, *Deaths and Entrances* means different things to different people. On one level it seems to be about the Brontë sisters. At the same time it can be seen as a study of the relationship between Martha and her own two sisters, Geordie and Mary, called "the Remembered Children" in the program. It also has been suggested that the work reflects a lonely struggle that was raging within Martha herself at the time, a conflict between her passion for Erick and her dedication to her art.

With its flashbacks and symbolism, *Deaths and Entrances* wasn't easy to follow. "At first seeing, it is perfectly safe to say that not a single spectator can honestly report that he knows what the work is all about, though it must be acknowledged that it is gripping and emotionally moving," wrote John Martin after the New York premiere. And critic Henry Simon said, "*Deaths and Entrances* is a long work . . . full of sound and fury, signifying something, but just what I do not feel able to say."

"The public seems baffled but moved in some way they do not understand," Martha wrote to David Zellmer. "I do not think I [would] understand it if I were asked to chart it completely. It just came that way." Graham believed that the secret emotional world made visible by a dancer's movements cannot always be expressed in words. She wanted her dances to be "felt" rather than "understood."

Years later, in an interview with dance critic Anna Kisselgoff, Martha said that *Deaths and Entrances* is "not a mirroring of my life" but speaks "to anyone who has a family." Kisselgoff called the dance a "modern psychological portrait of creative energy in women going to waste—of women unable to free themselves of themselves to follow their hearts' desires."

In Graham's next major work the heroine has no problem at all following her heart's desire. And this time the audience had no difficulty following the action.

Once again Martha paid tribute to her American heritage. *Appalachian Spring* takes place at a time when America was young, in the region where Martha spent her early years and where her Puritan ancestors first put down roots. With an arresting set by Isamu Noguchi that suggests an Appalachian homestead, and memorable music by Aaron Copland, the dance depicts a

Martha Graham and Erick Hawkins in *Appalachian Spring*, 1944, with May
O'Donnell in the chair at left and Yuriko and Nina Fonaroff in the background.
Photograph by Arnold Eagle.

pioneer celebration in spring as a bride and groom take possession of their
newly built farmhouse.

Appalachian Spring had its premiere at a Library of Congress concert on
December 30, 1944. Graham, who had turned fifty that year, danced the role
of the young bride. Hawkins portrayed her proud young farmer-husband.
Merce Cunningham, who would soon leave the company to form his own

modern dance troupe, was cast as a mesmerizing revivalist preacher. And May O'Donnell played a seasoned pioneer woman modeled on Graham's great-grandmother, who was "very beautiful and was always very still." Each of these characters dances a solo that expresses his or her personality traits and feelings. And as the work ends, the newlyweds are left alone in their farmhouse, quiet and strong, with the suggestion of a baby yet to come.

Martha as the bride in *Appalachian Spring*.

Appalachian Spring was an instant success. "Nothing Martha Graham has done before has had such deep joy about it," wrote John Martin, who added that Martha danced "like a sixteen-year-old." Aaron Copland's musical score earned him a Pulitzer Prize. And the dance itself became Graham's most popular and best-known work. She would continue to perform the role of the bride well into her sixties before finally relinquishing it to younger dancers.

The most lyrical of Graham's dances, *Appalachian Spring* expressed her growing love for Erick Hawkins. Agnes de Mille called the piece "a love letter, a dance of hope, budding, fresh, and beautiful." With its radiant optimism, this poetic and moving work sings of the promised joys of domestic bliss.

With dancers in her studio. Photograph by Barbara Morgan.

CHAPTER TEN

MAKING A $\mathcal{D}$ANCE

MARTHA'S DANCES DID NOT come easily to her. "However much people may help you," she said, "you are still a Viking on a ship going out to sea alone . . . when you are in the lonely and agonizing process of creating a new work."

The beginning of a dance, when the idea was just starting to take form, was "a time of great misery." Martha worked late into the night, propped up in bed, writing down thoughts, observations, impressions, quotations from books—anything that could help feed her imagination. "I would put a typewriter on a little table on my bed, bolster myself with pillows, and write all night."

"I get the ideas going. Then I write down, I copy out of any book that stimulates me at that time any quotation, and I keep it. And I put down the source. Then, when it comes to the actual work, I keep a complete record of the steps. I keep note of every dance I have. I don't have notation. I just put it down and know what the words mean, or what the movements mean and where you go and what you do and maybe an explanation here and there."

She read widely as she was searching for ideas and inspiration, studying psychology, yoga, poetry, the Greek myths, the Bible. She traveled regularly to the American Southwest and to Mexico, where she continued to be influenced by tribal rituals and ceremonies. And she looked deeply into herself.

She did not hesitate to borrow ideas: "I am a thief—and I am not ashamed. I steal from the best where it happens to be—Plato, Picasso, Bertram Ross. I am a thief—and I glory in it . . . . I think I know the value of what I steal and I treasure it for all time—not as a possession but as a heritage and a legacy."

Gradually the ideas that filled her notebooks would begin to reveal a pattern, and she would write out a detailed scenario or script. At that point she was ready to start work with a composer.

She wanted original music written especially for each new work. Often

Graham commissioned original music for many of her dances. Here she listens to a recording of a new score.

she would hand over her script to the composer before working out the actual dance steps. The script included notes and quotations from her reading, along with instructions concerning the placement of the dancers, the sequence of their movements, where there was to be a solo, a duet, or a dance for the entire company, and so on.

Graham's collaboration with Aaron Copland on *Appalachian Spring* is considered a landmark in the American theater. Much of the work was done through the mail, since Copland was living in Mexico at the time and Graham was traveling between New York, Bennington, and Washington. Several versions of the script went back and forth as Copland offered suggestions and Graham made revisions. Not until they were both satisfied did Copland actually compose the musical score. And only then, with the music in hand, did Graham begin to choreograph. Copland called his work "Ballet for Martha."

Martha's chief collaborator among stage designers was her good friend Isamu Noguchi. When she was developing a new idea, she would discuss it with him at length, often over the telephone, elaborating on the theme she had in mind, its origins, her special needs onstage, and so on. He would listen carefully, think deeply about the idea, then make a scale model of a set based on everything Martha had said. Some of his stage settings were strange sculptural forms that suggested mental and emotional states, the "inner landscape" that Graham was exploring.

When the scale model was ready, Noguchi would invite Martha to his studio. She would walk around the model, examine it, stare at it, touch it, and finally say, "Isamu, it's lovely, but I need time to think about it overnight."

The next day Isamu would phone Martha before she could call him and tell her that he had already changed his design. They knew each other so well, he was able to sense her reaction and respond to it immediately. "We worked together without problems," he said. "I felt that I was an extension of Martha, and that she was an extension of me."

Along with music and stage settings, lighting effects were extremely important to Graham. Until 1935, she personally designed the lighting for all of her dances. After that, she worked with several lighting directors, most notably Jean Rosenthal, who collaborated with Graham on thirty-six productions and, like Noguchi, became a close personal friend.

Then the dancers. Translating ideas into actual dance movements was always a cooperative undertaking. The original idea for a movement might be Martha's, but she needed her dancers' input to realize that idea. "The dancers might develop it, expand it," said dancer and choreographer Pearl Lang, "but she was there every second of the time, shaping, molding, modeling. Her hands were never off it, like a sculptor's."

Sometimes the movement she was searching for would not reveal itself. Martha would try one approach, then another, then stand silently at the stu-

Isamu Noguchi examines a model in his studio. He collaborated with Graham for more than half a century.

Lighting effects create a dramatic scene in *Frontier*. Photograph by Barbara Morgan.

dio window, staring out, thinking. The dancers would sit on the floor, waiting, until she turned to them and said, "Let's try this."

After a dance had been roughed out, Martha always turned to Louis for suggestions and criticism, counting on "his ferocious standards." Louis had an unerring eye for any movement that was not essential to a dance. He knew what to cut out, how to keep the piece focused. And he did not mince words.

Martha would flare up sometimes, throw a book or a shoe at Louis, beat him with her fists, storm out of the room. But she valued his honesty, and when she calmed down, she followed his advice. "I gave her discipline," he once said. "I was the tail to her kite, because she was a wild one . . . . I was her thread to earth."

Always a perfectionist, Martha was never satisfied. If a piece was only "nearly right," she would scrap it. She threw away much of what she had worked out. And when she bumped up against a creative block, she often lost patience.

Isamu Noguchi designed the set, the headdress, and the jewelry for Graham's 1950 solo, *Judith*.

"We used to watch her with alarm," Gertrude Shurr recalled. "She had her tantrums because she couldn't draw out of herself all of the devils she kept inside her. When she couldn't rid herself, cleanse herself, it was just frightful. Louis waited for the purge, when, and only when, would come her wonderful creativity. . . .

"I thought this was the way Martha had to be, because she wasn't a normal human being. She was a genius. We all knew that, and I think she knew it too. But, oh, she was so possessed!"

"I loved Erick very much. . . ." Photograph by Barbara Morgan.

CHAPTER ELEVEN

MARTHA *&* LOPES

OVER THE YEARS MARTHA CREATED many memorable roles for herself, ranging from the nameless figures in dances like *Heretic* and *Lamentation* to her psychological portraits of Emily Dickinson and Emily Brontë. During the 1940s she turned her attention to the larger-than-life heroines of Greek mythology, entering what many believe to be the most fruitful period of her career. Mythology happened to be a special interest of Erick's; he had studied the Greek classics as a student at Harvard University.

Martha wasn't concerned with a literal retelling of these ancient tales. Instead, her mythological heroines were meant to dramatize yearnings and emotions that are universal and that everyone can recognize.

All-consuming jealousy is the theme of *Cave of the Heart* (1946, music by Samuel Barber), the first dance-drama in Graham's Greek cycle. Martha danced the role of the sorceress Medea, who discovers that her husband, Jason, has been unfaithful. Driven to murderous revenge by her jealousy, Medea becomes the personification of hate. She kills her rival with a poisoned crown, then slays her own children and presents their bodies to Jason. In a chilling solo, danced partly on her knees and partly while squatting, Medea seems to devour a red snakelike ribbon, then spews it out of her mouth as though jealousy has turned her heart into a venomous serpent.

The unfaithful Jason was played by Erick. Medea's rival was danced by

Martha Graham as the sorceress Medea in *Cave of the Heart*, 1946.

Yuriko, a young Japanese American girl who had joined Martha's company after being released from a World War II internment camp. Graham was among the first in the world of dance to recruit Asians and blacks into her company, long before the civil rights movement.

Errand into the Maze (1947, music by Gian Carlo Menotti) deals with the need to conquer fear. This dance explores the legend of the Greek hero

Theseus, who journeys to the island of Crete to kill the Minotaur, a terrifying monster with the head of a bull and the body of a man. The Minotaur dwells deep inside a labyrinth, a winding, mazelike cave where he devours youths and maidens sent to him for sacrifice.

Graham danced the role of a female Theseus, representing anyone who ventures into a strange place in order to conquer deep-seated fears and doubts. In a thrilling ciimax she confronts the Creature of Fear and slays him, then escapes from the labyrinth by following a twisting white tape that symbolizes the maze.

Errand into the Maze, 1947. The twisting white tape symbolizes the maze leading to the Minotaur's lair.

"This dance has a special significance for me because it expresses the conquering of fear in my life, fear of the unknown, fear of something not quite recognizable," Graham said later.

By now Martha had become one of the biggest dance celebrities in America. Her New York performances often sold out, and her company's tours were under the management of the famous impresario Sol Hurok. After struggling for so many years, she began to live in a style befitting a star. In the past she had always bought her clothes at discount stores or made them herself. Now her good friend Bethsabee took her shopping and saw to it that Martha was outfitted in elegant designer dresses and hats. Eventually Martha moved to a nicer apartment, furnished it with antiques, and enjoyed the attentions of a cook and a maid.

In her personal life she was approaching a critical turning point. Martha and Louis had been working closely together for some thirty years, but their relationship had been under increasing strain ever since Erick had joined the company. Their intimacy was a thing of the past. Louis still presided as the company's musical director, but he resented Erick. And he was no longer at Martha's beck and call.

Martha's relationship with Erick, meanwhile, was anything but peaceful. Both of them were strong willed and egotistical, and their love affair was a stormy one. Martha seemed to fear that a deep emotional commitment would interfere with her life's work. But now Erick was an inseparable part of her life. "She was madly in love with him," wrote Agnes de Mille. "She had waited and he had come. He was the man for her."

During the summer of 1948 Martha was working on one of her lighter pieces, a joyful dance about the delights of love called *Diversions of Angels*, with a sprightly musical score by Norman dello Joio. Playful and exuberant, it joined *Appalachian Spring* as one of the few Graham dances that puzzled no one and delighted everyone on first viewing. It was also the first work in which Graham did not create a part for herself.

At a dress rehearsal for *Diversions of Angels* Martha criticized the way Louis was conducting the orchestra. Tempers flared, and angry words flew back and forth between the stage and the orchestra pit. The quarrel was brief, but it was a clear sign of the strain that had been creeping into their relationship. After conducting the premiere of *Diversions of Angels* in New London, Connecticut, Louis packed his bags and announced that he was leaving the company for good. Martha begged him to change his mind, but he refused. "I've turned over a page, and I'm not going to turn it back," he said.

Soon afterward Martha and Erick surprised everyone they knew by driving to Santa Fe, New Mexico, where they applied for a marriage license. They were married during a local fiesta by a Presbyterian minister in the foyer of his church. Martha held a bouquet of wildflowers and wore a little veil over her face. The only witnesses were the church organist and a close friend who lived in Santa Fe.

It was the first marriage for both. Erick was thirty-nine years old. Martha, who had always insisted that she would never marry, was fifty-four. When she filled out the marriage license, she deducted eight years and put down forty-six.

"I didn't want to [marry], but I did it," she said.

Martha Graham mending Erick Hawkins's pants.
Photograph by Barbara Morgan.

Ballerina Alicia Alonso congratulates Graham in her backstage
dressing room following a performance.

CHAPTER TWELVE

THE WORLD AT HER $\mathcal{F}$EET

"I LOVED ERICK VERY MUCH, not only physically, but also as a companion," Martha wrote in her autobiography. "And we were very happy . . . for a little while, until things became difficult."

After marrying in Santa Fe, they went camping at the Grand Canyon, where they cooked steaks over an open fire and slept under the stars. Back in New York Erick worked hard as the manager of Martha Graham and Company, raising funds, booking tours, and supervising rehearsals. Martha created some dances especially for him, and she encouraged him to choreograph solos for himself, but nothing Erick did on his own brought him the recognition he craved. When the critics panned his work, he felt that they were being prejudiced in Martha's favor. She dominated the company as always, while Erick remained in her shadow.

"Our marriage is a living thing, a give and take, what a marriage should be," Martha told Agnes de Mille. "But it is so difficult to make it work." Their relationship had been stormy from the beginning, and marriage did not make it any easier for these two temperamental artists to get along. At times their shouting matches could be heard all over the studio.

In the spring of 1950 the company sailed to Europe for its first prolonged international tour, with engagements in Paris and London. Martha was fifty-six and suffering from arthritis. To prepare for this important tour, she had pushed herself mercilessly, practicing and rehearsing until she strained the tendons in her legs.

Opening night in Paris was a gala event, attended by notables from all over Europe. Martha's reputation had preceded her, and the theater was filled to the last seat. A distinguished audience had come to see the best the United States had to offer.

The program that night featured four works. Martha danced in three of them. Toward the end of the evening, while dancing the role of the Empress of the Arena in *Every Soul Is a Circus*, she tore a cartilage in her knee and barely managed to finish her performance. By the time the curtain came down, her swollen knee was the size of a grapefruit.

Martha and Erick performed together for the last time in the 1950 Paris production of *Every Soul Is a Circus*. Photograph by Barbara Morgan.

The next day she could hardly walk. Erick pulled together a new program, and that evening Martha watched from the wings, leaning grimly on a cane as her dispirited dancers performed without her. When it was announced that the company's star was incapacitated, the Paris public stopped buying tickets. The rest of the engagement was canceled.

The company moved on to London. Martha tried out her leg and found that she was in no shape to dance there either. There are conflicting stories concerning what happened next, but it seems clear that Martha and Erick had a heated argument over whether or not to cancel the London engagement.

According to Jean Rosenthal, Graham's lighting director, Erick argued that the company should go ahead and perform in London without Martha. "He gave Martha the impression that he felt she wasn't necessary," said Rosenthal. "He probably didn't mean it, but that's the way it came out. I couldn't even begin to describe what Martha said and did. You wouldn't believe it. It was terrifying!"

When Erick suggested that Martha could sit on the sidelines, their marriage was doomed. "I was her equal," Hawkins said later, "and that created a lot of tension, which is why I left."

Martha saw things differently. "When it became clear that [the London season] would have to be canceled, Erick left me," she wrote. "He divided our money, left a note, and was gone."

That put an end to the company's European tour, and to Martha and Erick's marriage. Martha's young husband had walked out on her. Erick left the company for good to begin an independent career as a dancer, choreographer, and director of his own dance company.

"We had theater tickets that evening, and I met Martha during the intermission," dancer Ethel Winter recalled. "Now, she is a small woman, but she never gave the appearance of being small until that night. I never saw anyone look so devastated."

Martha went back to Santa Fe, stayed with friends, and nursed her injured leg and wounded pride in solitude. For a time she felt that she might never dance again.

Doctors advised surgery on her knee, but she refused. She was afraid that an operation might put a permanent end to her dancing career. Determined to rehabilitate the leg herself, she began to lift weights. "I started with very little weights," she recalled. "I got to where I could put a typewriter in a sling and lift it with my leg. When I was able to lift twenty-five pounds, I was healed."

It took a lot longer to heal her shattered emotions. "Erick and I had had a love affair, a very deep love affair," she wrote. "I never loved anybody but Erick in that way. It was difficult to get over it, but what choice did I have?"

Her salvation lay in her work. Six months after the failed European tour—"the accident," as she called it—she was back on the New York stage in a performance of *Judith* (music by William Schuman), a demanding twenty-minute solo inspired by the Jewish heroine in the Old Testament who murders a tyrant in order to save her people. A year later, in 1951, Graham created another long and difficult solo for herself with *The Triumph of St. Joan* (music by Norman dello Joio), a portrait of the French military leader and martyr Joan of Arc.

Martha had always created her dances as starring vehicles for herself, but for a few years she had been allowing leading members of her company to take over some of her roles. *The Triumph of St. Joan* marked the end of her unsupported solo days. Unhappy with her performance, she quietly decided that she could no longer hold the stage alone throughout an entire work. From then on she would rely on her dancers to support her as the central figure in a dance work.

She was having a hard time getting over Erick. Dancer and choreographer John Butler found her weeping alone in the studio one night: "I heard her sobbing. But it wasn't the crying of someone in grief or despair—it was something deeper, almost like a wounded animal in pain. There were torrents of tears, and her body was wracked with tension. It was extraordinary, like something from a Greek tragedy. I sat there for about two hours until her body calmed down and I felt I could leave."

Never again would Martha give herself so completely to another person. "There was never anyone after Erick," she said. "Perhaps there should have been. But there was not. There was no one."

Martha as the French martyr Joan of Arc in *The Triumph of St. Joan*, 1951.

Early in 1954 Martha and her company returned to Europe, this time for a triumphant tour that took them to several cities across the continent. Modern dance was looked upon as a uniquely American art, and as European audiences flocked to see America's most famous modern dancer, the U.S. State Department realized that Martha Graham was a valuable cultural resource.

In 1955 the government asked Graham to tour Asia and the Middle East. She became the first American dancer to travel abroad as a cultural ambassador. This trip lasted four months as the company of fourteen dancers and nine staff members visited major cities in Japan, the Philippines, Thailand, Indonesia, Burma, India, Iran, and Israel.

At each stop Martha gave lectures and press interviews. Nearly sixty-two now, she had the stamina to perform in two out of three dances on every program. "Though the rest of us wilt with the heat and sometimes drop out from dysentery, she never misses a performance," wrote Paul Taylor, one of the dancers on the tour who later became another dance legend.

Arriving in Tokyo during Graham's 1955 State Department tour of the Far East.

"She was just remarkable," Ethel Winter said. "She had to give speeches everywhere. Really, it was a thrill to be with her on that tour and see her in that light. She had a sense of what her mission was. It was really very marvelous."

Audiences in Asia were not familiar with the new art of modern dance, but they seemed to have no trouble enjoying Graham's dances. "They weren't shocked that we sat on the floor, that we rolled on the floor, that we danced barefoot," Bertram Ross remembered. "It was very understandable to them. Even if they had never seen modern dance before, they could relate instantly because of their own dance traditions."

It shouldn't be surprising. In those ancient Eastern countries, dance ceremonies dealing with gods and mortals, with the eternal conflicts of good and evil, and with the mysteries of the human heart have been part of culture and religion for thousands of years. Audiences in that part of the world could see those same dramas being played out as Martha's traveling troupe performed.

In fact, some Asian dancers have noted that Graham's approach, her way of moving, has much in common with the Eastern way of thinking about the body. According to choreographer Willy Tsao, founder of Hong Kong's pioneering City Contemporary Dance Company, "A Graham contraction is similar to the Chinese *chi-gong*, or breath-exercise, which is the foundation of the Chinese martial arts and also comes from deep inside the gut.

"The Chinese practice of *chi* is more internalized and less dramatic than a Graham contraction," said Tsao, "but they are both ways of harnessing a person's inner energy. Martha Graham was searching for a meaningful way of expression without knowing, perhaps, that in the East, many generations ago, there were also people searching for the same thing in a similar way."

State Department officials called Graham "the greatest single ambassador we have ever sent to Asia." In Tokyo the company gave four performances in a two-thousand-seat theater packed with standees. On closing

Martha meets a
Kabuki dancer
in Tokyo.

night the audience threw flowers and confetti on the stage and set off fire-crackers to honor the dancers. In Rangoon, Burma, the dancers performed on a specially constructed outdoor stage before crowds of four and five thousand. Many people in the audience brought food and cooked meals while waiting for the performance to begin. "I could smell the most marvelous curries while I danced Medea," Martha recalled.

With Erick gone, Martha was again personally managing her company and conducting rehearsals. She continued to create major works. And her teaching schedule was heavier than ever. In 1951 she had moved her rehearsal studio and dance classes to a handsome turn-of-the-century town house at 316 East Sixty-third Street, in Manhattan, which remains today the home of the Martha Graham Center for Contemporary Dance. And she

Students in a Graham class are made aware of the power of the spine.

continued to teach popular classes at the Juilliard School of Music, the Neighborhood Playhouse, and other schools and colleges.

Students described her as a tough but inspiring teacher. "The other teachers are great but they do not shoot electricity out of their eyes," said Robert Moulton, who studied with Graham in the 1950s. "She never tells you anything with just her mouth. No! She tells you with every fiber of her body."

The roster of Graham students and dancers who went on to form their own dance companies reads like a Who's Who of modern dance and includes dancers and choreographers as diverse as Merce Cunningham, Erick Hawkins, Pearl Lang, and Paul Taylor. The Graham technique, meanwhile, has influenced many other dancers and choreographers throughout the world.

Some of Graham's dance students have become famous in other fields, among them the pop diva Madonna, who enrolled in Martha's school before she became a celebrity. "I liked her tremendously," said Martha, who admired Madonna's sassy independence and forthrightness. "She was going to get what she wanted and to hell with everyone. Just like I was."

Graham's Movement for Actors classes at the Neighborhood Playhouse trained many young people who would someday become well-known Broadway and Hollywood personalities. Over the years her drama students included Oscar winners Bette Davis and Joanne Woodward, actor Gregory Peck, comedian and filmmaker Woody Allen, and musical comedy star Liza Minnelli.

One of Graham's colleagues at the Neighborhood Playhouse was the noted playwright Horton Foote, who worked with her on several student productions. "She made you feel as if you could take on the world," Foote remembered. "I've never been so charmed in all my life. She acted as if it were a great privilege to work with me. With me! Imagine! . . . After rehearsals we would get on a bus and we would ride together downtown to our homes. She would talk to me as if she had known me forever."

By the early 1950s Martha and Louis had reconciled and become supportive friends again. Martha phoned Louis regularly, invited him to watch rehearsals, and asked his advice. When he had a heart attack in 1955, she rushed to his bedside. By then, Louis had settled into a new relationship with a young dancer who cared for him dearly. Martha lived alone.

In 1958 Martha reached another landmark when she created and starred in *Clytemnestra*. With a score for voices and orchestra by the Egyptian composer Halim El-Dabh, settings by Isamu Noguchi, and lighting by Jean Rosenthal, this was one of the first evening-length works ever created in the

Martha Graham and Bertram Ross in *Clytemnestra*, 1958. Photograph by Arnold Eagle.

field of modern dance. Martha danced the title role, portraying the aging queen of Greek mythology, "an angry wild wicked woman," who looks back upon the crucial moments of her life to discover why she has been condemned to reside among the restless dead in Hell.

At the age of sixty-four Graham was no longer as agile as she once had been. To conserve her waning powers, she choreographed the three-act, three-hour dance-drama so that it could be acted as much as danced. Clytemnestra is constantly on stage, and while she is not always moving, she dominates the action as the other dancers move around her.

Arthritis had twisted Graham's hands into gnarled claws that she could neither open fully nor close tightly. She deliberately made those hands part of her portrayal. As the dance opened, she walked to the front of the stage and thrust her hands out toward the audience.

As the evil queen Martha held her audience rapt by imagination. Her masterful performance was hailed as one of her greatest triumphs, but at the same time it was a clear sign to her public, and to Martha herself, that she could not go on dancing forever.

Martha bares a crippled hand in her portrayal of the wicked queen Clytemnestra.

Taking a bow after a performance of *Legend of Judith*, 1962.

CHAPTER THIRTEEN

A TIME OF SNOW

FOR YEARS CRITICS HAD BEEN saying that Martha Graham was slowing down. Martha ignored them. She could no longer kick as high or move as fast as she might have wished, but she kept on dancing.

Others in her company had taken over some of the roles that Martha had made famous. And she was now creating major new roles for her leading female dancers, gifted younger women like Yuriko, Mary Hinkson, and Ethel Winter. But she wasn't willing to give up all her roles, or to choreograph only for others. Nothing could take the place of dancing herself. "It is all in life that has meaning for me," she said.

Between 1959 and 1969, her last full decade as an active performer, Graham created ten new roles for herself, along with eight additional new dances for her company in which she did not appear. As always, she seemed truly happy only when she was working.

Year after year the dances kept coming, full of surprises and new theatrical inventions. *Acrobats of God* (1960, music by Carlos Surinach) was a tribute to dancers—those "divine athletes," as Graham liked to call them— and a humorous spoof in which Martha poked fun at classical ballet, at modern dance, and at her own pretensions. In *Phaedra* (1962, music by Robert Starer), she turned again to Greek mythology, portraying the aging Cretan princess who falls tragically in love with her young stepson.

David Wood, Bertram Ross, Ethel Winter, and Martha Graham in *Acrobats of God*, 1960. Photograph by Martha Swope.

Phaedra caused an uproar when it was performed in Germany as part of the U.S. government's cultural exchange program. Two members of Congress, Representatives Edna Kelly of Brooklyn and Peter Frelinghuysen of New Jersey, walked out of the performance and denounced the work as shockingly erotic. They objected to the use of federal funds to help support such a production. And they urged that some form of censorship be imposed on art forms sponsored by the government and exported from America.

The two lawmakers were probably ignorant of the classic Greek legend that inspired Graham's version of *Phaedra* as well as other famous dramas written over the centuries. "We couldn't quite make it out," Frelinghuysen said, "but the import was clear." If the lawmakers had stayed to the end of the dance, they would have seen that the ancient legend delivers a stern moral when the erring princess is punished for her lust.

In Europe Graham found herself embroiled in a controversy over censorship and artistic freedom. She told reported that she would never do anything to embarrass her country. Back home leading figures in the American arts community rallied to her defense, praising her integrity and calling her the greatest artist American dance had ever produced. Meanwhile, all the publicity made *Phaedra* a sensational box-office hit as the public rushed to see what the excitement was all about. But if people expected pornography, they were disappointed to find in Graham's *Phaedra* a serious exploration of dark human passions, a disciplined and honest work of art.

Martha still dominated the stage when she performed, but she was mindful of her growing limitations. More and more she created roles that emphasized her acting gifts and personal magnetism but were less physically demanding. Onstage she sat or posed much of the time, portraying her character by means of gestures and facial expressions. Her friend, the actress Katharine Cornell, called Martha the greatest actress in America.

Graham made creative use of the flashback technique she had pioneered over the years. Many of her works deal with the ebb and flow of memory as the leading character remembers and acts out events in her past. In some of her later dances, a lithe and supple company member would emerge from the mists of the past to portray "the young Clytemnestra," or "the young Judith," while Martha, in the title role, stood regally at the edge of the stage or high upon a platform and watched her youthful self dance with glorious abandon. This allowed her to act out her role instead of fully dancing it.

During these years Graham's company was performing at a peak of speed, strength, and skill. "All of them, men and women, are beautiful to look at; all of them are trained to the state of ease in energy; all of them have an underlying dramatic awareness of what is going on about them; and all of them move as if they were sentient branches of Martha Graham herself," wrote John Martin.

Martha depended especially on her new leading man, Bertram Ross, who had started dancing at Graham's school under the G.I. Bill of Rights

Martha Graham rehearsing Mary Hinkson and Bertram Ross for the London premiere of *Circe*, 1963.

after serving in World War II. She would telephone Ross early in the morning or late at night to talk about changes and new ideas she had in mind, and he would meet her at the studio so they could work out the problem together. "I thought the company the most remarkable in the world," he said. "I loved them all."

Martha was proud of her superbly trained and resourceful dancers, and she intended to keep them that way. She was still a demanding taskmistress, as tough and uncompromising as ever.

"Martha challenged you to be her equal," said dancer Robert Cohan. "If you could do it, fine. If you couldn't do it, you failed. And if you failed, then she really couldn't be involved....While you were in the company, she would die for you. The moment you left, you were gone."

Like a tightrope walker Martha seemed to rely on tension. As the time for a performance approached, she felt compelled to keep herself and her dancers at a high pitch of nervous energy. She would deliberately stir things up. "If there wasn't something to be upset about, she would make something to be upset about," Ethel Winter recalled. "She needed this kind of tension, this kind of conflict, to go into performance. She did it just to get upset, just to get her blood going. Martha thrived in a crisis. It gave her energy."

"One of her methods was to pit dancer against dancer because she wanted a level of emotional involvement that she couldn't get just from rehearsing," said her friend Amy Kellman. "She'd tell one dancer one thing and another dancer another thing, and then she would get the kind of clash she wanted on stage. That animosity would come out in rehearsal, and she'd say, 'That's what I want!'"

If Martha could no longer fly across the stage, she still maintained a performing schedule that might have exhausted many younger women. Along with successful seasons in New York and regular cross-country tours, Graham's company visited Europe and the Middle East in 1962, 1963, and 1967, flying from place to place in two Constellation aircraft, one plane for the dancers, orchestra, and crew, the other for baggage and scenery. In Lisbon, Portugal, Martha performed *Clytemnestra* in an ancient bullring before a huge crowd that cheered her on with cries of *"Olé! Olé!"* She called that performance "the culminating moment of my life and career." She was seventy-three.

She kept busy, but she mourned her declining powers. Her arthritis was worse than ever, and when the disease flared up, she moved slowly and with pain. She wore elegant long gloves to hide her knotted and twisted hands. And with the loss of those people to whom she had been closest, she felt very much alone.

Martha's mother died in Santa Barbara in 1958. Louis Horst, her oldest friend, passed away in 1964. During his last illness Martha visited him often in the hospital, speaking to him in baby talk, scolding him like a little boy for getting ill. Barely able to reply, he admired the dress she was wearing. "It makes you look nineteen again," he told her. His death at the age of eighty deprived Martha of the one person she had trusted and respected throughout her career. "His sympathy and understanding, but primarily his faith, gave me a landscape to move in," she said. "Without it, I should certainly have been lost."

And there were other painful losses as well—the dying of old companions and collaborators, the departure of some of her best dancers as they left the company to pursue independent careers. Martha would call these years her time of "black despair." She suffered lengthy bouts of depression, brooding alone in her apartment and missing rehearsals. Enraged by the betrayal of her aging body, she began to drink heavily.

"It was no secret that Martha was relying somewhat more on alcohol to keep herself going, to dim her awful recognition of the fact that she must soon stop dancing," wrote critic Walter Terry, who had become a close friend. "Drink helped her to fool herself into believing that she could postpone the inevitable."

Martha's friends worried about her. And her dancers were terrified when she made her way onto the stage with glazed eyes and liquor on her breath.

By the late 1960s audiences were whispering that Martha Graham could no longer dance. Young people who knew the Graham legend, and went to see her for the first time, wondered what all the shouting was about. In their eyes Graham was an old lady who remained immobile on the stage as the action swirled around her. Critics complained that there was "more drama than dance" in her performances. "Why can't people accept what she is doing?" asked her friend the poet Ben Belitt. "She is brilliant. She is like light now. She makes you see what you are supposed to see."

She refused to quit. In 1968 she created new roles for herself in *A Time of Snow* (music by Norman dello Joio) and *The Lady of the House of Sleep* (music by Robert Starer), works that deal with age, sorrow, and longing. *A Time of Snow* tells the poignant tale of Abelard and Héloïse and their doomed love affair in medieval France. Martha portrayed Héloïse as an elderly nun. She looks back on her life as the young Héloïse of memory, played by Naomi Lapzeson, emerges from the mists of time and dances with fiery passion.

Bertram Ross as the monk Abelard and Martha Graham as the nun Héloïse in *A Time of Snow*, 1968.

Martha's friends tried to convince her that she did not need to dance any longer. She was still a brilliant choreographer, an inspiring teacher, a great actress. But she was determined to hang on as long as she could. "I'm a dancer and that's all I've ever been," she told them. "Take that away and there's nothing left."

Matters finally came to a head when members of her company demanded the right to perform without her. She was angered and hurt, and at first she resisted. But she knew in her heart that if her dances were to endure, she would have to give up to younger dancers the great roles she had created for herself.

In 1969 Martha Graham gave her last performance at the age of seventy-five. Later, she reluctantly announced her retirement. "The decision made

The Lady of the House of Sleep, 1968: Graham's last role as a dancer.

me physically ill," she said. "I had to retreat to the country until I made certain adjustments within myself. Someone told me, 'Martha, you are not a goddess. You must admit your mortality.' That's difficult when you see yourself as a goddess and behave like one. . . . In the end, I didn't want people to feel sorry for me. If I can't dance anymore, then I don't want to. Or at least I won't."

After her retirement Martha sank deeply into depression. "I had lost my will to live," she wrote. "I stayed home alone, ate very little, and drank too much and brooded. Finally my system just gave in."

She suffered a collapse that alarmed everyone who knew her. Gravely ill, she was hospitalized repeatedly, bedridden at home, and mired in apathy. She insisted that she had diverticulitis, an inflammation of the intestinal tract, but her friends were convinced that she was suffering from the long-term effects of alcoholism. For a time she was not expected to recover. She showed little interest in her company or school, and she did not set foot in her studio for nearly a year.

"Without dancing, I wished to die," she said. But she discovered that she was tougher than she realized, that nothing short of death could snuff out her creative urge.

In 1972, three years after her last public dance performance, Martha announced that she would reemerge as director of her company—a triumph over illness and despair that friends viewed as one of the greatest creative acts of her life.

Backstage.

After her retirement, Martha continued to supervise rehearsals and coach
individual dancers.

CHAPTER FOURTEEN

"I WOULD MUCH RATHER BE *Dancing*"

"IT IS A BITTER THING with me not to be able to dance again," Martha told a reporter after her retirement. She did not dance again, at least not in public, but she did make a spectacular comeback. Emerging from despair, she marched into her school, resumed her duties as its chief director, took charge of her company, and began to create new dances.

Except for New York's Metropolitan Opera, the Martha Graham Dance Company was now the single oldest existing theatrical institution in the country. Back on Broadway after an absence of four years, the company presented the premieres of two new Graham dances and revivals of some of her classics. "In the spring of 1973," wrote Walter Terry, "Martha Graham was reborn not simply for herself, but for us." The following year, with her eightieth birthday behind her, Martha set out with her dancers on a lengthy tour of Asia.

At her side was a young admirer, a former law student and photographer named Ronald Protas, who had come along at this time in her life to befriend and encourage her. He had worked hard to gain Martha's confidence and had been especially attentive during her illness. Once, while visiting her in the hospital, he had run to get help when Martha suddenly needed oxygen. She felt that Ron Protas had saved her life. From then on she relied on him, and he made himself indispensable to her.

When she returned to her company, she brought Protas along as her adviser and second in command. He would remain close to Martha for the rest of her life and, as Graham's heir, eventually take over as the company's artistic director.

"I have to give Ron Protas credit for bringing her back to life, because he really treated her like a princess or queen, a goddess, and she loved it," said Martha's friend Jeanette Roosevelt. "That was what fed her ego and got her back on her feet."

Protas had no experience as a dancer, choreographer, or administrator, however, and his new position of authority caused resentment among many of Graham's veteran dancers and associates. During a period of turmoil and recriminations, a number of key people left and the company was reorganized. Martha, it seems, wanted to start anew, with a clean slate. She wanted new dancers, new ideas, and new projects, and she distrusted anyone who opposed her.

Mary Hinkson and Bertram Ross, principal Graham dancers for many years, had kept the company and school going during Martha's absence. Both of them quit after the 1973 season. "Martha's attitude toward men and women and everything else was: they perform a service," said Ross. "Martha said, 'Bertram Ross is my skin,' and she wouldn't make a move without me. When you were no longer necessary, she would make you disposable."

"In retrospect, I can see that to be exposed to Martha was a singular, extraordinary experience, often very frightening, often terrifying, but certainly enriching," said Hinkson. "If you survived the experience, you would either come out stronger or defeated. The best thing that could happen was that you came out whole."

Still vigorous in her eighties, Martha taught classes at her school almost daily. She supervised rehearsals, coached individual dancers, reconstructed some of her older masterworks, and continued to choreograph new works. "I would much rather be dancing," she confessed. "I will always miss it."

When dancer Tim Wengerd arrived early for a rehearsal one day, he found Martha in the studio alone, weeping. "She did not try to hide it," he recalled, "but said that she had dreamed that night that she was dancing, and then she awoke and saw her cruelly twisted hands and realized she would never dance again. This woman was almost eighty years old, and what she wanted to do most was dance."

The dances that Graham created after her retirement rarely focused on a strong central character. She found it too painful to place in the body of another dancer the same movements and roles she once would have brought to life herself.

She had always thought of herself as a performer, not a choreographer. "I never cared much for choreography," she said. "I think I only started to choreograph so that I could have something to show off in. It came as a great shock to me when I stopped dancing that I was honored for my choreography as well."

Eighty-year-old Martha Graham arrives in Burma on her company's 1974 Far Eastern tour.

The spunky young rebel who had challenged the dance establishment with shocking solos like *Revolt* was now the grand old lady of contemporary dance. After her return to work in 1973 Graham created over twenty new works and thirty major revivals. And if her new dances were no longer as daring or innovative as many of her earlier works, she was recognized as one of the century's great artistic pioneers, often compared to Pablo Picasso and Igor Stravinsky, her counterparts in painting and music. Students came from all over the world to study at her school. Some of the finest dancers of the time came to learn her dances. Martha was now part of the establishment she had once defied. She had become a world-renowned institution.

Honors and awards were heaped upon her. She received honorary degrees from Yale and Harvard, the key to the city of Paris, and Japan's Imperial Order of the Precious Butterfly. In 1976 she became the first person from the field of dance to receive the Presidential Medal of Freedom, American's highest civilian honor. Placing the medal around Martha's neck at a White House ceremony, President Gerald R. Ford, whose wife Betty had studied with Graham, called Martha "a national treasure."

Graham's reputation as a visionary artist attracted superstars from the world of classical ballet who wanted to work with her. Rudolf Nureyev, the fiery Russian-born dancer and choreographer, worshiped Graham and haunted her company's performances. In 1975 Nureyev and Margot Fonteyn, the celebrated British ballerina, performed with the Martha Graham Dance Company in *Lucifer* (music by Halim El-Dabh), a work that Martha had choreographed especially for the two stars. Mikhail Baryshnikov, another famous Russian-born ballet star, later teamed with Nureyev to star in a revival of *Appalachian Spring*. And in 1978 musical comedy star Liza Minnelli took the speaking role in *The Owl-and the Pussycat* (music by Carlos Surinach), a comic parody of Graham classics based on Edward Lear's nonsense poem.

While Martha no longer danced, she continued to appear onstage in the popular lecture-demonstrations that she had developed into an art form. A striking figure with a gaunt face like a primitive mask, a seductive voice, and a faultless sense of timing, she still knew how to hold an audience spellbound.

(*above*) Watching
a rehearsal.

(*left*) Liza Minnelli
and Martha Graham
on the set of *The Owl
and the Pussycat*, 1978.

Rudolf Nureyev and Martha Graham on stage following a performance at the Paris Opera House, 1984.

As she talked about her life and work, young dancers demonstrated her techniques.

More than ever, there was little room in Martha's life for anything that detracted from her intense devotion to the dance. Her work was her reason for being. "She does not have in her life, nor did she ever have, what other women have in the way of shared love, shared responsibility, shared growth," dancer and choreographer Sophie Maslow observed. "But maybe she gets the same fulfillment in life in her artistic growth, her artistic status."

After her breakup with Erick, Martha had seriously considered adopting a child, but she had long since given up any such idea. "I chose not to have children for the simple reason that I felt I could never give a child the caring upbringing which I had as a child," she wrote. "I couldn't control being a dancer. I knew I had to choose between a child and dance, and I chose dance."

Her legendary status in the world of dance and her great age seemed to place her on a lonely and windswept plane. She lived alone in an elegant apartment a short distance from her school. And she traveled in style, escorted everywhere by Ron Protas and outfitted in regal splendor by her good friend the fashion designer Halston. "I am elderly," she admitted. "I am old, and if I dress my age I will look older than God's aunt, and I don't want to look that old. In fact, I refuse to, so I choose to be flamboyant."

The dances kept coming—a dozen new works during the last decade of her life. *Acts of Light* (1981, music by Carl Nielsen), one of her most beautiful works, is a moving meditation on love and loss and a celebration of the life-giving powers of the sun. Martha took the title from a line in one of Emily Dickinson's letters: "Thank you for all the acts of light which beautified a summer now past its reward."

Graham's last complete work, composed when she was ninety-six years old, is one of her most joyful. *Maple Leaf Rag* had its premiere in New

Pop diva Madonna greets her former dance teacher at the premiere of Martha Graham's 180th work, *Maple Leaf Rag*, 1990.

Martha Graham and her company. Photograph by Martha Swope.

York's City Center theater on October 13, 1990. A self-mocking commentary on human foibles and on her own legend, the work is set to the ragtime tunes of Scott Joplin, the music that Louis Horst had played to cheer up his "Mirthless Martha" more than half a century before. The dance begins with a recording of Martha's voice saying, "Oh, Louis, play me the 'Maple Leaf Rag.'"

Martha traveled abroad with her company several times when she was in her eighties and nineties. In the fall of 1990 she set out on a fifty-five-day tour of the Far East. As usual, she intended to accompany her dancers each step of the way, to share everything with them.

She still looked forward to her curtain calls. While she didn't perform, and could hardly walk, she would appear onstage every night for a bow at the end of the evening's show. First the dancers would come out for their curtain calls. Then the curtain would come down and Martha would be helped out to center stage. When the curtain rose again, she would be seen standing there, proud and erect, wrapped in a shimmering Halston gown, glowing like a polished porcelain doll. She gloried in that fleeting moment when the audience rose cheering to its feet.

Back in New York after the Asian tour, Martha came down with pneumonia. She never recovered. She died at home on April 1, 1991, a few weeks shy of her ninety-seventh birthday. The front-page *New York Times* headline read: MARTHA GRAHAM DIES AT 96: A REVOLUTIONARY IN DANCE.

At the time of her death she was working on a new dance, commissioned by the government of Spain to celebrate the five hundredth anniversary of Columbus's voyages to America. She called the new work *The Eyes of the Goddess*, or a "journey through time."

The Russian novelist Feodor Dostoyevsky once said of Columbus that he did not set out to discover the New World, but himself. We could say the same for Martha Graham. By trying to discover herself, she found the New World of Modern Dance.

During her own long journey, she created 181 original dances, many of them lasting works of art. And she invented a new way of moving, a unique dance language that has thrilled audiences all over the world and enlarged our understanding of what it means to be human.

Dancer and choreographer Lila York has called Graham "a heroine of the twentieth century, an example of courage and independence. She was an exemplary artist who told us: 'Yes, you can take chances with your life, you can take a stand for what you are, what you believe in, and what you care about; one thing will follow another, and you'll make a life for yourself.'"

Acclaimed as a great choreographer, Martha always insisted that she wanted to be remembered first as a *dancer*. "Many people have asked me if I have a favorite role," she said. "To which I always answer that my favorite role is the one I am dancing now."

Photograph by Barbara Morgan.

NOTES

Unless otherwise noted, references are to books and articles cited in the bibliography; Louis Horst's taped interviews with Jeanette Schlottman Roosevelt, 1960–1961; and interviews with the author.

Chapter 1: Acrobats of God

Graham, "Finally, I learned how to walk . . ." is from Graham, 1991a, p. 103.

Graham, "Stand up! . . ." is quoted in de Mille, 1991a, p. 102.

Graham, "I don't call myself a choreographer . . ." is from the Graham interview in Horosko, 1991a, p. 11.

Ross, "Here was somebody . . ." is from an interview with the author, 12/10/96.

Ross, "At my very first class . . ." is from an interview with the author, 12/10/96.

Graham, "I did not choose . . ." is from Graham, 1965, p. 54.

Tetley, "When I first saw . . ." is quoted in de Mille, 1991a, p. 333.

Chapter 2: Bewitched by the Goddess

George Graham, "Martha, you're not telling me the truth . . ." is quoted in Terry, 1975, p. 1 and in Stodelle, 1984, p. 2. Martha Graham told this story many times over the years, and while the details differed, the essential facts remained the same.

Graham's grandmother, "I would rather . . ." is quoted in Graham, 1991, p. 25.

Graham, "I was a very difficult child . . ." is quoted in Terry, 1975, p. 8.

Graham, "I was quite stubborn . . ." is from Graham, 1991, p. 23.

Graham, "I always wanted . . ." is from the PBS video documentary, *Martha Graham: The Dancer Revealed,* 1994.

Graham, "a place of ceremony . . ." is from Graham, 1991, p. 35.

Graham, "spun entirely out of evening . . ." is from Graham, 1991, p. 30.

Graham, "Freedom! I ran . . ." is quoted in Stodelle, 1984, p. 7.

Graham, "I was not the pretty one" is quoted in McDonagh, 1973, p. 15.

Graham, "From that moment on . . ." is quoted in McDonagh, 1973, p. 16.

Graham, "We were left . . ." is from Graham, 1991, p. 60.

Graham, "She became very excited . . ." is from Graham, 1991, p. 58.

Chapter 3: Going to the Top

St. Denis, "You take her . . ." is quoted in Terry, 1975, p. 27.

Shawn, "She was quite a few years . . ." is quoted in de Mille, 1991a, p. 52.

St. Denis, "She was exceedingly quiet . . ." is quoted in George M. Douglas, *Women of the Twenties* (Dallas, Texas: Saybrook Publishers, 1986), p. 99.

Graham, "trying to find strange, beautiful movements . . ." is from Graham, 1991, p. 67.

Graham, "They thought I was good enough . . ." is from Graham, 1991, p. 66.

Shawn, "It's too bad . . ." is quoted in Terry, 1975, p. 32. For differing versions of Graham's first performance of *Serenata Morisca* see Stodelle, 1984, p. 26; de Mille, 1991a, p. 53; and Graham, 1991, p. 68.

Shawn, "Sometimes my face . . ." is quoted in Terry, 1975, p. 37.

Graham, "I was like an animal . . ." is from Graham, 1991, p. 79.

Tacoma New Tribune review, "a brilliant young dancer," is quoted in Stodelle, 1984, p. 32.

Graham, "I could not do anything . . ." is quoted in McDonagh, 1973, p. 29.

Douglas, "She would take out easy steps..." is quoted in Stodelle, 1984, p. 32.

Graham, "I had a very bad temper . . ." is from Graham, 1991, p. 82.

Shawn, "I don't ever . . ." is quoted in de Mille, 1991a, p. 66.

Graham, "this huge, great-spirited musician . . ." is from Graham, 1991, p. 74.

Graham, "He encouraged . . ." is from Graham, 1991, p. 74.

Graham, "Louis brought me out . . ." is quoted in Kisselgoff, "Martha Graham," 1984, p. 54.

Graham, "The *Follies* served a purpose . . ." is from Graham, 1991, p. 103.

Graham, "I'm going to the top . . ." is quoted in Terry, 1975, p. 42.

Chapter 4: Revolt

Graham, "a word I never heard of . . ." is from Graham, 1991, p. 69.

Graham, "I nearly fainted . . ." is from Graham, 1991, p. 98.

Horst, "I began talking . . ." is from Horst's interviews with Roosevelt.

Graham, "I wanted to gamble . . ." is from Graham, 1991, p. 110.

Graham, "They came because . . ." is from Graham, 1991, p. 110.

Newspaper reviews, "decorative, pretty and undisturbing . . ." are quoted from Gardner, 1993, p. 271.

Graham, "childish things, dreadful" is quoted in McDonagh, 1973, p. 50.

Horst, "With these dances . . ." is from Horst's interviews with Roosevelt.

Horst, "I can't explain . . ." is from Horst's interviews with Roosevelt.

Marchowsky, "What a disciplinarian . . ." is from Horosko, 1991a, p. 66.

Horst, "We were always together . . ." is from Horst's interviews with Roosevelt.

De Mille, "This was a stirring period . . ." is from Agnes de Mille, *Dance to the Piper* (Boston: Little, Brown, 1951), p. 114.

Horst, "They were experimenting . . ." is from Horst's interviews with Roosevelt.

Shurr, "All I can remember . . ." is from Horosko, 1991a, p. 34.

Fisher, "We didn't expect to be paid . . ." is quoted in de Mille, 1991a, p. 130.

Horst, "When she's down . . ." is from Horst's interviews with Roosevelt.

Graham, "Oh, Louis . . ." is from Graham, 1991, p. 274.

Martin review, "strikingly original . . ." is quoted in de Mille, 1991a, p. 89.

Graham, "To many people . . ." is from Graham, 1991, p. 114.

Martin, "Audiences who come . . ." is quoted in Armitage, 1966, p. 8.

Young, "She looks as though . . ." is quoted in de Mille, 1991a, p. 122.

Actress friend, "Martha, how long . . ." is quoted in Terry, 1975, p. 61.

Graham, "I wanted people to like me . . ." is quoted in Terry, 1975, p. 57.

Chapter 5: Creating a New Language of Dance

Graham, "Dance is another way . . ." is quoted in Mazo, 1985, p. 61.

Graham, "My quarrel . . ." is quoted in Terry, 1975, p. 61.

De Mille, "not so much a crashing down . . ." is from de Mille, 1991a, p. 100.

Graham, "The floor is a direction . . ." is quoted in Terry, 1975, p. 53.

Horst, "That was the first . . ." is from Horst's interviews with Roosevelt.

Schonberg, "Of course, when we all sat . . ." is from Mazo, 1991, p. 39.

Woman in audience, "You will never know . . ." is quoted in Graham, 1991, p. 117.

Chapter 6: Testing the Limits

Graham, "Now, let's see you . . ." is quoted in de Mille, 1991a, p. 215.

Graham's movement images, see Graham, 1991, pp. 252–53.

Graham, "Movement in modern dance . . ." is quoted in Stodelle, 1984, p. 56.

Bird, "Everybody was hypnotized . . ." is quoted in de Mille, 1991a, p. 130.

Graham, "Wherever a dancer stands ready . . ." is quoted in de Mille, 1991b, p. 22.

Graham, "Sit down with me here" is quoted in Stodelle, 1984, p. 111.

Graham, "He became my lover . . ." is quoted in Kisselgoff, 1984, p. 54.

Horst, "Why *that* movement? . . ." is quoted in Stodelle, 1984, p. 50.

Graham, "But Louis, you're destroying the idea . . ." is quoted in de Mille, 1991a, p. 109.

Graham, "You're putting out the fire" is quoted in Stodelle, 1984, p. 72.

Martin, "No other dancer . . ." is quoted in Gardner, 1993, p. 276.

Terry, "Innocent people . . ." is from Terry, 1975, p. 78.

Graham, "That's enough! . . ." is quoted in de Mille, 1991a, p. 181.

Watkins review, "The most significant choreography . . ." is quoted in Gardner, 1993, p. 282.

Graham, "It was so striking . . ." is from Graham, 1991, p. 143.

Chapter 7: New Frontiers

Graham, "a wonderful place . . ." is from Graham, 1991, p. 162.

Stodelle, "Up the winding road . . ." is from Stodelle, 1984, p. 95.

Graham, "The American dancer . . ." is from Armitage, 1966, p. 107.

Terry, "I was there . . ." is from Terry, 1975, p. 80.

Graham, "It was a terrible performance . . ." is quoted in Stodelle, 1984, p. 98.

Martin, "She is a genius . . ." is quoted in de Mille, 1991a, p. 233.

De Mille, "She was great fun . . ." is from de Mille, 1991a, p. 151.

Graham's visit to the White House is from Horst's interviews with Roosevelt and from Graham, 1991, p. 151.

Graham, "It never entered my mind . . ." is from Graham, 1991, p. 151.

Graham's letter to Goebbels is quoted in McDonagh, 1973, p. 113.

Graham, "Do you think . . ." is from Graham, 1991, p. 151.

Graham, "I took it . . ." is from Graham, 1991, p. 151.

Chapter 8: Enter Erick

Hawkins, "My being a man . . ." is from Mazo, 1991, p. 42.

Graham, "I'm afraid . . ." is quoted in Terry, 1975, p. 61.

Graham, "Now that we modern dancers . . ." is quoted in McDonagh, 1973, p. 148.

Martin, "Better let it sleep . . ." is quoted in Stodelle, 1984, p. 114.

Martin, "one of the most beautiful . . ." is quoted in de Mille, 1991a, p. 244.

Graham, "Sometimes a dance . . ." is from Graham, 1991, p. 115.

Graham, "If I were to take that step . . ." is quoted in de Mille, 1991a, p. 239.

Chapter 9: A Love Letter

Horst, "but emotionally . . ." is from Horst's interviews with Roosevelt.

Maslow, "I remember speaking . . ." is quoted in de Mille, 1991a, p. 249.

Graham, "I wish I could say . . ." is quoted in Aloff, 1995, p. 36.

Keller, "What is jumping?" is quoted in Graham, 1991, p. 148.

Martin, "At first seeing . . ." is quoted in de Mille, 1991a, p. 252.

Simon, "*Deaths and Entrances* is a long work . . ." is quoted in Gardner, 1993, p. 296.

Graham, "The public seems baffled . . ." is quoted in Aloff, 1995, p. 36.

Graham, "not a mirroring of my life" is quoted in Kisselgoff, 1984, p. 54.

Graham, "very beautiful and was always very still" is from Graham, 1991, p. 232.

Martin, "Nothing Martha Graham has done . . ." is quoted in de Mille, 1991a, p. 261.

De Mille, "a love letter . . ." is from de Mille, 1991a, p. 261.

Chapter 10: Making a Dance

Graham, "However much people may help . . ." is quoted in Terry, 1975, p. 155.

Graham, "I would put a typewriter . . ." is quoted in Kisselgoff, 1984, p. 52.

Graham, "I get the ideas going. . . ." is quoted in McDonagh, 1973, p. 161.

Graham, "I am a thief . . ." is from Graham, 1973, p. xi.

Graham, "Isamu, it's lovely . . ." is from Graham, 1991, p. 222.

Noguchi, "We worked together . . ." is quoted in Stodelle, 1984, p. 153.

Lang, "The dancers might develop it . . ." is quoted in de Mille, 1991a, p. 138.

Horst, "I gave her discipline . . ." is quoted in de Mille, 1991a, p. 362.

Shurr, "We used to watch her . . ." is quoted in de Mille, 1991a, p. 146.

Chapter 11: Martha Elopes

Graham, "This dance has a special significance . . ." is from the PBS video documentary, *Martha Graham: The Dancer Revealed,* 1994.

De Mille, "She was madly in love . . ." is from de Mille, 1991a, p. 231.

Horst, "I've turned over a page . . ." is from Horst's interviews with Roosevelt.

Graham, "I didn't want to . . ." is from Graham, p. 174.

Chapter 12: The World at Her Feet

Graham, "I loved Erick . . ." is from Graham, 1991, p. 174.

Graham, "Our marriage . . ." is quoted in de Mille, 1991a, p. 285.

Rosenthal, "He gave Martha . . ." is quoted in Terry, 1975, p. 112.

Hawkins, "I was her equal . . ." is from Tracy and Kaye, 1991, p. 46.

Graham, "When it became clear . . ." is from Graham, 1991, p. 185.

Winter, "We had theater tickets . . ." is from an interview with the author, 12/11/96.

Graham, "I started. . ." is quoted in Terry, 1975, p. 113.

Graham, "Erick and I . . ." is from Graham, 1991, p. 186.

Butler, "I heard her sobbing . . ." is quoted in Horosko, 1991b, p. 46.

Graham, "There was never anyone . . ." is from Graham, 1991, p. 200.

Taylor, "Though the rest of us . . ." is from Paul Taylor, *Private Domain* (San Francisco: North Point Press, 1988), p. 66.

Winter, "She was just remarkable . . ." is from an interview with the author, 12/11/96.

Ross, "They weren't shocked . . ." is from an interview with the author, 12/10/96.

Tsao, "A Graham contraction . . ." is from an interview with the author, 1/14/96.

State Department officials, "the greatest . . ." is quoted in Stodelle, 1984, p. 179.

Graham, "I could smell . . ." is from Graham, 1991, p. 206.

Moulton, "The other teachers are great . . ." is quoted in de Mille, 1991a, p. 216.

Graham, "I liked her tremendously . . ." is quoted in the *Martha Graham Centennial* program, 1994, p. 10.

Foote, "She made you feel . . ." is quoted in de Mille, 1991a, p. 352.

Chapter 13: A Time of Snow

Graham, "It is all in life . . ." is quoted in de Mille, 1991a, p. 378.

Frelinghuysen, "We couldn't quite make it out . . ." is quoted in the *New York Times,* September 10, 1963, and the New York *Herald Tribune,* September 10, 1963.

Martin, "All of them . . ." is quoted in Stodelle, 1984, p. 218.

Ross, "I thought the company . . ." is quoted in de Mille, 1991a, p. 375.

Cohan, "Martha challenged you . . ." is from Tracy and Kaye, 1991, p. 46.

Winter, "If there wasn't something . . ." is from an interview with the author, 12/11/96.

Kellman, "She'd tell one dancer . . ." is from an interview with the author, 1/23/96.

Graham, "the culminating moment . . ." is quoted in de Mille, 1991a, p. 371.

Horst, "It makes you look . . ." is from de Mille, 1991a, p. 361.

Graham, "His sympathy . . ." is quoted in de Mille, 1991a, p. 362.

Terry, "It was no secret . . ." is from Terry, 1975, p. 132.

Belitt, "Why can't people . . ." is quoted in Stodelle, 1984, p. 236.

Graham, "I'm a dancer . . ." is quoted in Terry, 1975, p. 133.

Graham, "The decision . . ." is quoted in Gardner, 1993, p. 304.

Graham, "I had lost my will . . ." is from Graham, 1991, p. 237.

Graham, "Without dancing . . ." is from Graham, 1991, p. 238.

Chapter 14: I Would Much Rather Be Dancing

Graham, "It is a bitter thing . . ." is quoted in Stodelle, 1984, p. 256.

Terry, "In the spring . . ." is quoted in Stodelle, 1984, p. 261.

Roosevelt, "I have to give . . ." is from an interview with the author, 9/27/96.

Ross, "Martha's attitude . . ." is from Tracy and Kaye, 1991, p. 44.

Hinkson, "In retrospect . . ." is from Tracy and Kaye, 1991, p. 46.

Graham, "I would much rather be dancing," is quoted in Tracy and Kaye, 1991, p. 44.

Wengerd, "She did not try . . ." is from Wengerd, 1991, p. 49.

Graham, "I never cared . . ." is from Graham, 1991, p. 236.

Maslow, "She does not have . . ." is quoted in de Mille, 1991a, p. 236.

Graham, "I chose not to have children . . ." is from Graham, 1991, p. 160.

Graham, "I am elderly . . ." is quoted in de Mille, 1991a, p. 421.

York, "a heroine . . ." is from an interview with the author, 2/14/97.

Graham, "Many people have asked . . ." is from Graham, 1991, p. 255.

ACKNOWLEDGMENTS

The following people—dancers as well as colleagues, associates, and friends of Martha Graham—generously gave their time in interviews for this book. I am grateful to them all for their insights, anecdotes, descriptions, explanations, and opinions:

William Batcheldor, Philip Grosser, Amy Kellman, Daniel Maloney, Jeanette Schlottman Roosevelt, Bertram Ross, Willy Tsao, Ruth Westerman, Ethel Winter, Lila York.

Special thanks to Jeanette Schlottman Roosevelt for allowing me to read and quote from the unpublished transcripts of her 1960–1961 taped interviews with Louis Horst.

I am indebted to Jack Anderson and George Dorris for their comments and suggestions on my manuscript, and to Evans Chan, Phil Gerrard, Isabella Halsted, Carolyn Goor Hutchinson, and Susan Pine, who shared their knowledge of and enthusiasm for dance with me, and who helped arrange interviews.

For help in obtaining photographs, I want to thank Dorothy Eagle, Reiko Sunami Kopelson, and Lloyd Morgan; also, Allison Bergman of the American Foundation for the Blind and Amy Hau of the Isamu Noguchi Foundation.

This book could not have been written without the resources of the Dance Collection at the New York Public Library for the Performing Arts at Lincoln Center. My gratitude to Monica Mosely, Madeleine M. Nichols, Charles Perrier, and the other staff members who assisted me.

—R.F.

PICTURE CREDITS

The photographs in this book are from the following sources and are used by permission and through the courtesy of the copyright owners:

American Foundation for the Blind, Helen Keller Archives: 96

AP/Wide World Photos: 143 top, 145

Photographs by Arnold Eagle; courtesy of Dorothy Eagle: 99, 126

Photographs by Barbara Morgan; Morgan Press, courtesy of Lloyd Morgan: 2, 13, 54, 57, 58, 69 bottom, 72, 75, 76, 80, 82, 84, 86, 87, 88, 90, 92, 97, 102, 107, 110, 115, 118, 152

Isamu Noguchi Foundation, Inc.: 106

Photographs by Martha Swope; © Time Inc.: 130, 146

Photographs by Soichi Sunami; Dance Collection, the New York Public Library for the Performing Arts; Astor, Lenox, and Tilden Foundations; courtesy of Reiko Kopelson: 43, 45, 49, 52, 60, 61, 64, 69 top

All other images are reproduced by courtesy of the Dance Collection, the New York Public Library for the Performing Arts, Astor, Lenox, and Tilden Foundations.

SELECTED BIBLIOGRAPHY

Books About and by Martha Graham

ARMITAGE, MERLE, ED. *Martha Graham.* Brooklyn, N.Y.: Dance Horizons, 1966. Brief articles by critics, collaborators, and friends on Graham's early years as a dancer and choreographer. Originally published in 1937 as the first book on Martha Graham.

DE MILLE, AGNES. *Martha: The Life and Work of Martha Graham.* New York: Random House, 1991a. Vivid, opinionated, and engrossing, this insider's account of Graham's personal and professional life is filled with anecdotes and gossip. A comprehensive biography by a fellow dancer, choreographer, and friend who knew Graham for nearly sixty years.

GARDNER, HOWARD. *Creating Minds: An Anatomy of Creativity Seen Through the Lives of Freud, Einstein, Picasso, Stravinsky, Eliot, Graham, and Gandhi.* New York: Basic Books, 1993. Graham is the only woman discussed in this scholarly look at the creative personality and the process of creativity.

GARFUNKEL, TRUDY. *The Life and Dances of Martha Graham.* Boston: Little, Brown, 1995. A concise, readable account for young people.

GRAHAM, MARTHA. *Blood Memory.* New York: Doubleday, 1991. Graham's own highly selective account of her life and career, published the year she died. Includes anecdotes, observations, and personal judgments not found elsewhere.

————. *The Notebooks of Martha Graham*. Edited by Nancy Wilson Ross. New York: Harcourt Brace, 1973. A dizzying array of thoughts and observations, trial scenarios, sequences of dance steps, occasional diagrams and drawings, and quotations from the literary and philosophical sources that inspired Graham. Difficult reading, sometimes incomprehensible, but offers insights into Graham's mind at work.

HELPERN, ALICE. *The Technique of Martha Graham*. Dobbs Ferry, N.Y.: Morgan and Morgan, 1994. A detailed account of Graham's dance technique and classwork with vintage photographs by Barbara Morgan.

HOROSKO, MARIAN. *Martha Graham: The Evolution of Her Dance Theory and Training, 1926–1991*. Pennington, N.J. and Chicago: Chicago Review Press, 1991a. Twenty-five dancers who worked with Graham over the years offer first-hand accounts of her training methods, her achievement, and her personality. Based on a day-long seminar held at the New York Public Library for the Performing Arts.

LEATHERMAN, LEROY, with photographs by Martha Swope. *Martha Graham: Portrait of the Lady as an Artist*. New York: Alfred A. Knopf, 1966. Includes a text by Graham's personal manager for many years and almost two hundred performance photographs taken during the 1950s and 1960s.

MCDONAGH, DON. *Martha Graham: A Biography*. New York: Praeger, 1973. Published nearly two decades before her death, this was the first full-length account of Graham's life and work. Based on public and private records and personal interviews, it remains the most carefully documented biography of Graham.

MORGAN, BARBARA. *Martha Graham: Sixteen Dances in Photographs*. Dobbs Ferry, N.Y.: Morgan and Morgan, 1980. Revised edition of a 1941 classic that includes many beautiful and dramatic action photographs of Graham in performance.

PRATT, PAMELA BRYANT. *The Importance of Martha Graham*. San Diego: Lucent Books, 1995. A biography for young people.

SOARES, JANET MANSFIELD. *Louis Horst: Musician in a Dancer's World*. Durham, N.C.: Duke University Press, 1992. The first full-length biography of Graham's lifelong mentor, ally, and confidant.

STODELLE, ERNESTINE. *Deep Song: The Dance Story of Martha Graham*. New York: Schirmer Books, 1984. A biographical study of Graham's performing and choreographic achievements, emphasizing her artistic development and creative process. Includes detailed descriptions of all major works.

TERRY, WALTER. *Frontiers of Dance: The Life of Martha Graham*. New York: Thomas Y Crowell, 1975. An engaging biography for young people by a dance critic and personal friend of Graham's.

Books About Dance

ANDERSON, JACK. *Ballet and Modern Dance: A Concise History*. Second Edition. Princeton, N.J.: Princeton Book Company, 1992. An entertaining and comprehensive history by a dance critic for *The New York Times*. Includes excerpts from primary sources and a section of biographical profiles.

DENBY, EDWIN. *Dance Writings*. Edited by Robert Cornfield and William MacKay. New York: Alfred A. Knopf, 1986. Essays and reviews by one of the most influential dance critics of this century. Includes reviews of sixteen Martha Graham dances.

JOWITT, DEBORAH. *Time and the Dancing Image*. Berkeley: University of California Press, 1988. A cultural history of dance by a critic for *The Village Voice*.

MCDONAGH, DON. *The Complete Guide to Modern Dance*. Garden City, N.Y.: 1976. By a dance critic for *The New York Times* and a biographer of Martha Graham.

MAZO, JOSEPH H. *Prime Movers: The Makers of Modern Dance in America*. New York: William Morrow, 1977. A dance critic discusses the lives and works of artists from Isadora Duncan to Twyla Tharp.

Magazine and Newspaper Articles

ALOFF, MINDY. "Family Values." *The New Republic,* September 11, 1995, pp. 30–36.

DE MILLE, AGNES. "Measuring the Steps of a Giant." *The New York Times,* April 7, 1991b, sec. 2, pp. 1, 22.

DUFFY, MARTHA. "The Deity of Modern Dance." *Time,* April 15, 1991, p. 69.

GRAHAM, MARTHA. "How I Became a Dancer." *Saturday Review,* August 28, 1965, p. 54.

————. "Martha Graham Reflects on Her Art and a Life in Dance." *The New York Times,* March 31, 1985, sec. 2, pp. 1, 8.

HARDY, CAMILLE. "Martha Graham, American Pioneer." *Dance Magazine,* June 1991, pp. 18–19.

HOROSKO, MARIAN. "Martha's Prince." *Dance Magazine,* June 1991b, pp. 46–47.

KISSELGOFF, ANNA. "Martha Graham." *The New York Times Magazine,* February 19, 1984, pp. 44–55.

————. "Martha Graham Dies at 96: A Revolutionary in Dance." *The New York Times,* April 2, 1991, pp. A1, B7.

MAZO, JOSEPH H. "Martha Graham." *Horizon,* 1985, pp. 57–64.

————. "Martha Remembered." *Dance Magazine,* July 1991, pp. 34–45.

ROBERTSON, NAN. "Martha Graham Dances With the Future." *The New York Times,* October 2, 1988, sec. 2, pp. 1, 26.

SHAPIRO, LAURA. "Graph of the Heart: Martha Graham Gave Dance a New Vocabulary." *Newsweek,* April 15, 1991, p. 77.

TRACY, ROBERT AND ELIZABETH KAYE. "I See You as a Goddess." *Mirabella,* July 1991, pp. 42–46.

TYNAN, KENNETH. "High Priestess of Modernism." *London Observer,* April 7, 1991, p. 59. Reprint of a 1963 profile.

WENGERD, TIM. "Martha's Men." *Dance Magazine,* July 1991, pp. 48–52.

Films and Videos

For a listing and discussion of films and videos about Martha Graham, see VIRGINIA BROOKS, "Martha on Film," *Dance Magazine,* July 1991, pp. 62–63.

ABOUT THE AUTHOR

RUSSELL FREEDMAN grew up in San Francisco and graduated from the University of California at Berkeley. After serving with the Second Infantry Division during the Korean War, he worked as a reporter and editor for The Associated Press, and later as a publicist for several network television shows. His first book, *Teenagers Who Made History,* was published in 1961.

A full-time writer ever since, Mr. Freedman is the author of over forty nonfiction books on subjects ranging from animal behavior to American history. His acclaimed titles include *Lincoln: A Photobiography,* the 1988 Newbery Medal Book; *The Wright Brothers: How They Invented the Airplane,* a 1992 Newbery Honor Book; *Eleanor Roosevelt: A Life of Discovery,* a 1994 Newbery Honor Book; and *Kids at Work: Lewis Hine and the Crusade Against Child Labor,* a 1995 Orbis Pictus Honor Book. Russell Freedman lives in New York City.